Surviving my Mother

How I Let Go of My Past to Reclaim My Soul and My Future

DEBBIE MATZKIN

Producer & International Distributor
eBookPro Publishing
www.ebook-pro.com

SURVIVING MY MOTHER

Debbie Matzkin

ISBN 9798388586346

Surviving my Mother

How I Let Go of My Past and Reclaimed My Soul and My Future

CONTENTS

To the reader

When a mutual friend referred Debbie Matzkin to me for counselling, we embarked upon a journey together to intensify her spiritual understanding. In time, we discussed the manuscript of the book Debbie had written several years earlier describing her life story and her insights on reaching inner peace. As she progressed in her therapy, she began to better understand her life lessons and to observe the changes. At that point, she asked me as her spiritual counselor and healer to join in the writing process to inject and intensify the spiritual understanding elements within the text.

Debbie has been developing her spirit and healing her human wounds in order to better herself and give the best of herself to others. She is now sharing her story to offer others a glimpse of her life and the inspiration to traverse their own path with confidence and meaning.

It has been my honor to walk this path with Debbie, especially when recalling her painful memories and sharing her pain and tears, as well as the relief she has reached through experiencing this process. I admire her bravery and the importance of the therapies she has experienced to now share her story out of joy.

I thank Debbie for this opportunity, and thank Melanie Rosenberg, the editor.

May all you be blessed.
With love,
Valda Tair Ozeri
Spiritual counselor, practitioner and teacher for the
emotional development of human consciousness

Introduction

Before we embark on our journey together, let me tell you who I am.

I'm a simple human being who, through the years, has learned what life is really all about.

I'm a little girl that developed into a woman who learned to forgive – not forget – but forgive, from the depth of my soul, all those who harmed me. And along the way, learned to be thankful for the lessons they gave me.

I'm a little girl who went through hell and through this journey discovered incredible things. Incredible places. Incredible cultures meshed within fascinating pieces of history.

I'm a person who grew up helpless under the dark ugly shadow of abuse. For too many years, I carefully hid terrible secrets deep inside me. Buried so deep that no one suspected that behind my wonderful family, possessions and career, lay a past riddled with unspeakable pain. Only my incessant nightmares pointed their shaky finger at me, giving me no peace.

It took time. But thanks to my own perseverance and my passion to soar (no matter how far below I'd plunged), I sought help in the most profound way through a process that involves the cleansing of body and soul. I first set about to heal my body from all the scars and toxins I'd ingested throughout my life. After a complete body detoxification, I moved to cleanse my soul from the beginning of time till what it is today.

In that process, I found myself, my soul, and who I really am.

Now, I am the happiest woman alive.

Through this book, I hope to teach women and men of all ages what I have learned: to respect each other, but mainly to respect yourself. For the very moment that you can respect yourself, you will learn to respect others. You will learn to understand others. You will learn not to judge, because judging takes you nowhere but to hurting yourself.

I want to give you a glimpse of the extraordinary people and places I've encountered along my journey.

Ultimately, my story proves that it doesn't matter where you come from in order to understand who you are and your place in this world. My dream is that through this book, I can help others understand who they are and find their purpose in life. May my story spur you to go for your dream and never give up! The first step is to heal the wounds of your past.

Come with me now along the travels I've taken to reach my soul. Your own journey of discovery is yet to come.

Debbie Matzkin

PART I:
The Journey Begins

I wasn't at all surprised when a sudden storm pierced the heavens that day, the day I told my family my real identity.

Showers pelted the rugged Miami sand to a white polish as I shut the bay window in the living room. Turning ever so slowly to face them, I announced, "You need to know who your wife is, and who your mother is." The firmness I heard in my voice sounded so unfamiliar. Did they sense this as well?

"I don't have time, Mom," my younger daughter said too quickly.

"I don't want to hear," my older daughter whispered.

"We know it all, of course," my husband assured me.

"Sit down," I said without flinching. "Sit down and listen to who I am and who I've been. This is the first time I'm telling the truth. It's not easy."

That's when the sudden roar of thunder shook the room. In a way, it gave me the strength to say: "The woman you're looking at was abused. Physically, mentally, emotionally and sexually abused. By my own mother. By Nana, who was not at all the caring person you thought she was."

Slowly, painfully I spoke of the torture, the horrible details that I'd kept secret, even to myself, for so many years. The frightened, confused and lonely child that was me, Debbie, emerged just as I'd left her so many years ago. But I kept talking until I'd said it all.

My daughters were visibly shocked.

"My children," I said, "When I cry to you, when I ask you to please love me, this means that I'm turning to you because I have no one else, just the two of you, who are

12

the lights of my life. I am the proudest of being your own mother.

"You have given me the strength to believe that I'm loved and protected by the Almighty. His gift to me is the power to go on."

They came and hugged me and they were crying. My husband didn't say a word.

And so began the best years of my life.

I

1963: Bogota, Columbia – Opening the Front Door

The cold, rainy season seemed endless and the skies were overcast from carrying such heavy, tired clouds. I was a child in my favorite room (not my bedroom; I was beaten there) in our enormous, elegant home. I was in the library. I guess, for me, this was the place where I came to hide.

What a magic place!

If I stood on my tiptoes, I could just reach the long shelves lined with a record collection of stellar performances by the world's finest concert musicians. (In my teenage years, I'd also reach for Tom Jones records and the latest American hits that had reached Colombia.)

Once the music filled the room, it was time to choose a book from the hundreds of volumes that surrounded me like a fortress. No matter how often I looked over the phenomenal assortment of English, Spanish, French, and German literature my parents had amassed, I was drawn like a magnet to the thick black volume I loved the most: *The Count of Monte Cristo* by Alexandre Dumas. Better than any of the movie versions I had ever seen, I kept replaying in my mind the vivid scenes I envisioned of Edmond Dantes' search for revenge. Turning the pages furiously, I'd meticulously plan my own sweet revenge on all of the people who did me wrong. Of course, the revenge Edmond achieved brought him satisfaction, but no inner peace. It is only now that I know that my own inner peace is my own true revenge.

The music and books were ideal for transporting someone as miserable as me to the delicious fantasy world I'd so carefully created. But getting there depended on my luck in grasping the one forbidden item that I'd risk everything for, time and time again.

The front door clicked firmly shut in the distance. As the car's motor began to purr, the garage door creaked open. True music to my ears! My mother had left the house. Now, to just wait for the housekeepers to turn their backs and go off and tidy up the kitchen.

Deftly evading their gaze, I crept up to Mother's room. In the dark I'd open her closet and run my hand through the wardrobe till I found the prize: Mother's magnificent eggshell-white Indian robe, woven with gold thread.

Treasure in hand, I was free to race back to my library hideaway to gloriously wrap the robe around me. Now, at last, I could choose a symphony to play, close my eyes, and twirl the fantasy gown as I danced and dreamed. Once again, my imagination saved me. And the wealth of books overflowing the library's polished oak shelves became the source of my knowledge of the world.

The Palace That Was My Home

The magnificent 14,000-square-foot home where I grew up dripped with the finest furnishings, paintings and sculptures from all over the world, perfect to the last touch. Yet nobody in all of Bogota knew how rotten this house was from within.

I was just two months old in 1956 when my parents brought me from New York to Colombia, where I grew up. We first lived in a small apartment, just 900 square feet, and then my mother decided she wanted to move to Bogota's newest neighborhood.

Mother had studied architecture at New York University, but I'm not sure if she ever graduated. The closest she ever came to working in that profession was when she undertook the project of designing our new house. She called a friend from New York to ask his help, who was happy to oblige. He also happened to be the son of Frank Lloyd Wright. Thanks to him, the house boasted a huge Wright-style entrance that opened to a formal living room, accented by a massive carpet interwoven with golden threads.

I was four years old when we moved into my mother's dream house, an elaborate palatial structure which quickly turned into my own personal torture chamber. Thinking back, I don't recall my mother ever abusing me outside of this home, or anywhere in the world on our many excursions. Only in that house did she feel safe, protected and free to beat the crap out of me.

Like my parents, I grew up in a home that was run by a twelve-man staff of housekeepers, including a cook, butler, gardener, driver, cleaners and others who maintained our home to perfection. For me, some of them were also the angels who would shower me with love.

These were men and women from little towns and villages in Colombia who flocked to the city to earn a meager wage. We paid them around $30 a month, as I recall. They used to work six days a week, but we were never without a housekeeper. Of course, "the help" were never allowed to sit at the same table with us. They also had their own quarters.

I was far too young (and too lonely) to obey the strict Colombian rules against interacting with the help. I would come and sit in the kitchen as often as I could, just to be with them and talk to them. I was allowed to receive their love, but never to be their friend.

We had a housekeeper, Claudina, who was with the family for forty-eight years. Then there was the cook, Lola, who was with us for twenty-seven years. She was an amazing person, and in essence she learned everything about cooking from my mother, who was indeed a master of the culinary arts.

In stark contrast to my own mother, Lola loved me intensely and took great delight in playing with me. While she was cooking, she'd sweep me up in her arms and coax me to eat. No matter what, she could always calm me down with a dish of spaghetti and chicken. Ironing with Lola was the best: She would take a sheet and set up a tent beside her, just for me and my dolls. Sometimes she would even crawl inside to play.

I must have been about ten or eleven years old when I realized that Claudina and Lola were illiterate. So, I decided to teach them how to read and write, and was transformed into a child-teacher without even trying. My father was convinced that I should take up a career in teaching.

(Did Claudina and Lola see my bruises and scars from the beatings? Did they suspect what Mother was doing to me? From the moment I was able, I never let anyone into the shower with me. I heal very well.)

Now, over fifty years later, something remarkable happened: A Facebook message arrived asking, "Do you know Lola Cordozo? She used to work in your house. I'm her goddaughter."

I responded immediately, and was thrilled to hear that Lola was alive and relatively well. The next day I carefully dialed the telephone number I was given for Lola, took a deep breath and said, "This is la nina Debbie." We both burst into tears. I've always loved her so!

In December 2019, I returned for a visit to Colombia. Here I finally had the opportunity to visit dear family members, and even to say good-bye to two wonderful relatives who died shortly afterwards. Almost miraculously, I was able to rekindle my precious acquaintance with Lola, who had the given me the warmth I longed for. I nearly cried when she proudly showed me an album she'd saved for some six decades, filled with photos of me as a little girl. What's more, she'd even kept the books I had given to teach her to read. "I never forgot you," she told me. "Every single night, all these years, I've prayed to God to protect you."

To my mother's credit, our help were held in high re-gard. One thing my mother did teach me was to treat everyone—a king or a homeless pauper—with respect.

For my part, until the day I left home in my late teens, I was never allowed to make my own bed or even to pick up my underwear. Nothing. My laundry was always done; my clothes were put away neatly in my closet. When I'd return home from school, my room was perfectly spotless.

Living a Charmed Life (Or So It Seemed)

Each evening, my father, my mother and I ate formal dinners in our massive dining room. We would take our seats at the long, stately table so elegantly graced by a white tablecloth, an exquisite fresh flower arrange-ment, and a formal table setting for three.

Our housekeepers were there on 24-hour call, dressed in their crisply- starched uniforms and aprons. Every dinner was French-served, with the food served from the right and lifted off the table from the left.

We always dressed for dinner. (You could never come in your pajamas.) Mother planned the menu each day and prepared the food, assisted by the cook and sous chefs. We began our meal with sliced melon or other fresh fruit, or perhaps a hearty soup. The main course was always freshly cooked – never leftovers. I can close my eyes this minute and still taste the succulent roast beef and rice that was my mother's famous specialty. And I looked forward to the sponge cake that came for dessert.

Dinner was conducted in a very formal manner, as Father demanded. I'll never forget the first time I slouched at the table. Father immediately stood up, strode to the medicine cabinet and pulled out some type of gauze bandage tape. He secured a stick behind my back as he wrapped the tape around me and said, "This is the way you're always going to sit at the table." That taught me to sit properly, henceforth and forevermore. You will never find me crossing my legs or putting my hands on the table. I have exceedingly proper seating and table manners, thanks to my father.

Every Wednesday afternoon when I'd come home from school, my culinary horizons would expand. Our Wednesday family ritual prescribed that my grandparents, my Uncle Lazar, my parents and I would go out to eat in a restaurant, come rain or shine.

Bogota boasted an extremely high standard of dining. From my earliest childhood, I literally cut my teeth on some of the finest food at some of Colombia's most amazing restaurants. My mouth still waters at the memory of the freshly-grilled fish that we would order at an elegant downtown French restaurant called "Eduardo."

Fishing was another family ritual. Every Wednesday and Sunday at 4:30 AM, my father, grandfather and Uncle Lazar would make a beeline to the lagoons outside of Bogota, where they would go trout fishing. The driver won the task of cleaning the fish that were reeled in, and the cooks would later prepare every trout dish imaginable for us to feast upon.

Then too, there was not a Sunday when my parents and I didn't go out as a threesome. Much of the time we stayed in Bogota, one of the most beautiful cities in the world. Often we'd have picnics with my parents' friends and their children, but there were also times when we would travel an hour to get to a particular restaurant nestled in the Colombian mountains or valleys. I can remember my father at the wheel of his Fiat 2000, Oldsmobile, Cadillac, or beige-colored Dodge, smiling as he whisked us off to another Sunday adventure.

Anyone who saw our little family—my tall, always impeccably-dressed father, my exceedingly cultured mother, and the carefree-looking child that was me—would surely see a paragon of a model family. But only I knew the dark side, the opposite of a light caressing touch of a mother's love that would never be mine to feel.

II

1969, Bogota, Colombia – A Terrible Secret

My best friend Ruthy Sherman came to my house to spend the weekend. We were thirteen years old and both puzzle buffs. Ruthy and I took advantage of the hot, sultry Saturday weather to hole up in the breezy library and set to work on a "killer" jigsaw puzzle with 1800 tiny pieces, creating an intricate landscape scene. When Ruthy finally slid the very last puzzle piece in place, we laughed and did a crazy victory dance.

It was nearly midnight when we went to sleep in adjoining bedrooms.

That night in my dream, the landscape scene came alive. I was running through a field of wildflowers, trying to find the bluebells that had made up such a beautiful left-hand corner in the puzzle. Carefree, I skipped along through cascades of flowers until I caught sight of them in the distance – a plush carpet of violet-hued bluebells nodding in the breeze.

But as I took a step forward, heavy vines suddenly rose from the brush to twist and tangle themselves around me, tighter and tighter. I struggled to wrest myself free, but nothing stopped the horrible, stifling torture. In a moment, I felt a heavy force crushing my face, strangling me, suffocating me, killing me. I was helpless to fight.

"Anita, stop it now! What are you doing? Let Debbie go!" I heard Ruthy shout shrilly at my mother.

Wide awake now, I opened my eyes to see my mother

lying across my chest, brutally crushing my face with a pillow. There was no air to breathe and no mercy in her twisted face as she kept pressing me, smothering me with all her might.

Ruthy began hitting my mother, desperately trying to break her death hold on my face. In what seemed like an eternity, Mother straightened up, lifted the pillow, and walked slowly out of the room. She did not look back or speak to either of us.

There was shock and fear in Ruthy's eyes as she tried to calm me. She hugged me as we cried together.

"It's okay, Debbie. I'm here to save you. I'll never leave you alone with her. I'll sleep here every single weekend forever! I won't let her try to murder you again!"

But I had an even worse fear.

"You must promise me that you will never, ever tell a soul what happened here," I whispered, pressing her hand to my heart.

"I understand," she said softly. "I promise."

I kept my promise. This has been my secret for most of my life. I never told anyone, so as not to shame my mother or to be gripped by the consuming fear of her retaliation.

***

A Word from the Therapist

A child cannot see the parent as an enemy, and may even come to think that abuse is normal behavior. We children take responsibility for our parents, keeping their secrets of behavior. We protect them, and sometimes even sacrifice ourselves for them.

As the behavior recurs, a vicious circle is created. The patterns of our youth can continue for a lifetime.

Debbie:

The trauma of my childhood taught me that I didn't want to be abandoned by people. I needed reassurance from the outside world that I was OK. As a child, I pleased my friends so they would say, "I love you." But even then, I was being abused by my classmates.

Therapist Arian Lev, internationally recognized expert on the subconscious:

Debbie's life was a recurring nightmare. Her mother abused her. Her mother's severe distress at her unwanted pregnancy was projected prenatally via gentle vibrational energy. At the embryonic stage, Debbie already perceived this message via a type of DNA code: I=delete. From birth, the command to delete herself only grew within her.

Ignored by a mother who didn't see her, Debbie felt alone. To her, love meant abandonment. Even though she was only a child, she should have been a princess, yet they didn't see her. She was here and she wasn't there.

She disconnected in order to survive.

She disappeared by entering an imaginary world.

When punished, she didn't feel the pain. Through protection behavior, she developed a way to protect herself until she "reprogrammed" her DNA.

As an adult, Debbie attracted friends, yet she couldn't see them as they were. She saw them living in her own bubble. From the womb, she perceived the disconnection between herself and her mother.

During the therapy process, as someone who had seen herself till now as I=Delete, Debbie learned to see the people in front of her and determine who was good and not good. Today she is free to release the barrier.

Mother, Grandma Golda
and Grandpa Ezekiel

"Debbie, your mother didn't really love you. She looked at you as an enemy who shouldn't be there, and she was quick to admit that to everyone. She loved her flowers more than she loved you."

Ruthy Sherman, 2015

It's true, really. Flowers were my mother's love and her passion. Mother's touch transformed the simplest blooms to some of the most exquisite floral arrangements I've seen to this day. She was the master of every floral array, from the disciplined delicacy of the Japanese Ikebana style to a chic, romantic French bouquet of roses. An all-star winner in flower competitions throughout Colombia, Mother was even cited for glory with the "Anita Rose," a special variety of rose that was officially named in her honor. This white rose was surrounded by pink and dark petals on the outside. Magnificent!

Anita Finkelman was a well-known active figure in Bogota's Jewish and non-Jewish social scene. For decades, she took the lead in the city's National Women's Club, in dynamic contact with the wives of the diplomatic corps stationed in Colombia, and jet-setting the world on her own as well. Within the Jewish community, she and her mother established the first WIZO (Women's International Zionist Organization) chapter in Colombia, which grew and thrived under Mother's guiding hand. For hobbies, Mother was a fervent Petit Point devotee whose works of fine stitches in canvas decorated every room in our home. She was also a nearly-addicted card player.

But above all, my mother was the quintessential hostess whose dinner parties were legendary in Bogota. Like her parents, Mother had a dining room table that comfortably seated up to twenty-four people. Although my grandmother's table extended to reach that size, Mother's table was one extremely long, one-piece wooden work of art. Around it stood beautiful, majestic chairs with vibrant emerald green and gold upholstery accentuating their graceful design.

It goes without saying that Mother had a full household staff at her disposal. She carefully instructed the housekeepers how to set the table and how to serve the meals with flawless precision. Mother did cook, but she always had a sous chef on hand to slice and prepare the raw ingredients. She never had to clean up the kitchen, nor did I once see her lift a dish to wash.

Regardless of the number of guests, Mother's meals were always served to perfection. Her zeal for travelling the world came straight to her table in a host of exotic dishes that she always brought home. Mother's French, Italian, and Oriental cooking creations, to name but a few, were a cause for celebration.

So why did this talented, successful, highly-respected woman abuse her only child? Beyond the premise that my birth was the unhappy result of an unwanted pregnancy, I sometimes suspect that my mother, too, was unloved as a youngster. She came from parents who belonged to Colombia's high society, and she was raised by nannies. My grandfather was a businessman who cared only about the business. My grandmother cared only about what society said, and gave nothing to her children. And who knows about their own upbringing? Psychologists have told me that it takes three generations to break the cycle of abuse, so that provided me a clue to start to understand.

Perhaps my mother was mentally ill? I know now that her own brother was manic depressive. Or did the head injury she suffered in an automobile accident when I was a teenager intensify her violence towards me? These questions haunt me to this minute.

Mother was born in Palestine in 1930. Her parents, Ezekiel and Golda Finkelman, had left their home and family in Chortkov, Poland just one year beforehand, as ominous turmoil befell the Jewish community and the gates to immigration were closing shut. Soon after my mother's birth, they set out from the Middle East on an epic voyage to Colombia, which I'll soon describe. Suffice it to say that my grandparents became extremely wealthy in this South American haven.

My mother grew up in a palatial home in the city of Cali, southwest of Bogota. I'm not sure if she ever felt welcome in her own home. When she was nine, her brother was born, immediately becoming the apple of his mother's eye. Then their younger sister was born, becoming the apple of her father's eye. My grandparents may well have looked upon my mother as a burden, the child that they had to bring from Europe: a reminder of their less-prestigious past.

At the age of thirteen or so, Mother's parents packed her up and sent her away to live and study in the nearby

Jesus Sacred Heart boarding school, which was run by nuns. She stayed there until her graduation. Like me, she was given no warmth whatsoever....

I understand that when Mother was accepted to the renowned New York University's Department of Architecture, her parents were dead set against the endeavor and refused to pay her tuition or expenses. Her Uncle Lazar, whom you'll meet soon, was the saint who came to the rescue to fund his favorite niece's education in America. Thanks to him, Mother was able to set out 2,500 miles from home as a woman on her own pursuing the complexities of architectural studies.

Although love and marriage soon took her three times farther away to live in Haifa, Israel, Mother eventually made her way back home to Bogota when I was just an infant. She then held the distinction of being one of the first women in the Jewish community of Colombia to have graduated from architectural school.

By Divine grace, we lived near her parents, who may not have overly loved my mother, but they adored me with a passion. Ultimately, it was the love of my grandparents and my aunt that saved my body and soul.

The Rise of the Finkelman Empire

If you stood at just the right spot in the breathtakingly beautiful mountains, you could peer deep into the valley below and catch a glimpse of the two famed bends in the Seret River that crisscrossed the city of Chortkov at two different points. But the best scenery was right before your eyes: the lush, verdant forests whose thick rows of lofty trees covered the mountains in shaded wonder.

For the Finkelman family, whose genealogical roots in the Chortkov area (in today's Ukraine) can be traced to at least the early 1800s, the forests – and precisely their trees – held a treasure as opulent as jewels.

For two generations, the Finkelmans were renowned as the most prominent lumber merchants in the entire region. My cousin Yaron Reshef, whose book *Out of the Shoebox* recounts his family research and recent journey to Chortkov, describes the once-thriving commerce of the Finkelman industrial empire. Their substantial import-export operation involved shipping massive logs from near and far to the Finkelman sawmills in Chortkov and nearby Jagnielnika. Here the lumber was sawed into custom-sized planks ordered by a client base extending throughout Galicia.

My grandfather Ezekiel (Yechezkel) and his four siblings grew up in the lap of (relative) luxury in Chortkov, then part of the Austrian Empire. Yaron actually found their spacious home still standing, which he described as an "architectural gem."

My great-grandfather Isaac and his wife Rifka Drucker Finkelman were both born in neighboring towns of Chortkov in the 1860s. Although Isaac and Rifka were not particularly orthodox, they did belong to a local synagogue whose spiritual leader Rabbi Yeshayahu-Meir Shapira was quite enlightened for his day. Rabbi Shapira championed both Zionism as well as the importance of continuing children's education beyond secondary school.

Thanks to Rabbi Shapira's inspiration and to the family's comfortable financial situation, my grandfather and his siblings were provided with a fine higher education. All the more rare and remarkable for the early twentieth century is that my great-grandparents permitted their two daughters to leave home to pursue their studies. My grandfather's sister Sima (Simka) completed medical school, and their sister Zelda was a philosophy student.

As for their Zionist fervor, the Finkelman youth were all active in the Betar Zionist Movement and developed a true penchant for Zionist ideals. My grandfather settled in Israel for a period in the 1920s, my uncle Shalom Zvi immigrated there in 1932, and my Aunt Simka (whom I resemble) immigrated in 1935. Her story is particularly tragic, for Simka returned to Chortkow the following year out of her devotion to serve the town's medical needs. In 1942, she, my great-grandmother Rifka, and the overwhelming majority of the large Chortkov Jewish community were herded onto trains bound for slaughter in the Belzec Death Camp.

Grandfather married Golda Schoenberg, daughter of Abraham and my namesake Devorah Buxbaum Schoenberg. Golda was born in the *shtetl* of Skala, adjacent to Chortkov. Golda's older brother Lazar Schoenberg joined her and Grandfather when they were living in Palestine as newlyweds, and he consequently accompanied them when they went to settle in Colombia.

Uncle Lazar was one of the most wonderful people I ever loved. Although he remained a bachelor, he was the person who grounded our entire family. I can never forget the way Uncle Lazar would drink tea: He would place his cup in a sterling silver holder. To his left were sugar cubes. With dexterity, Lazar would take a sugar cube, put it in his mouth, and then sip the glass of tea. So extremely elegant...

Although he worked in the Finkelman family business in Colombia until his death, I recently discovered that Lazar Schoenberg was actually a chemist by profession. Rumor has it that he personally provided Pedro Domecq with one of the formulas for rum.

***

Once they determined that it was time to leave Palestine and seek their fortunes elsewhere in the world, my grandparents and Uncle Lazar earnestly deliberated the whereabouts of their next destination. The winning locale was the metropolis of New York. With my infant mother in tow, the family made their way to a ship bound for the United States and South America. At some point along the voyage, my grandfather and Uncle Lazar became friendly with a fellow traveler by the last name of Burstein, who soon cast his lot with the Finkelman contingent.

Unfortunately, just as the Statue of Liberty came into sight in the glittering New York harbor, my grandfather was informed that he was being detained aboard ship because he lacked a proper visa to enter the United States.

With no better strategy at hand, the five remained floating at sea until the ship's next scheduled stop, Cuba. Supposedly, my grandfather was put off by the extreme heat roasting Cuba at the time, so he bid that country *adios* and the group continued to the ship's last stop, the exotic South American shores of Colombia.

Here these wandering Jews finally settled in the city of Cali, a prime economic center in Southwestern Colombia and the only major city in the country with access to the Pacific coast. Even though my grandfather and his two partners knew no Spanish and had no existing connections in the Colombian business world, they made it big. The three men literally descended to the salt mines to exploit this valuable Colombian commodity. Within a relatively short time, they rose to become major salt exporters to the world at large.

My grandparents were also among the first Ashkenazi Jews to reach Cali in the early 1930s, and soon became pillars of Cali's growing Jewish community. In a remarkably short time, the Finkelman family thrived.

By the time my parents and I moved to Colombia, soon after my birth in New York in 1956, my grandparents resided in the capital city of Bogota, where we joined them. Once again, my Grandfather Ezekiel had worked his financial wizardry, this time by selling the salt export operation in Cali to obtain funds for establishing a steel import enterprise in Bogota. My Uncle Lazar remained his steadfast business partner in *Finkelman and Schoenberg, Ltd.*, and my father eventually entered the business as well. In time, they became the largest importers of construction steel in all of Colombia.

I never cease to marvel at how my grandfather left the lumber export business of Poland to build a prosperous Colombian salt export company as well as a booming business in steel imports. True, fate brought him to Colombia at a particularly propitious time in the nation's economic development. Opportunities abounded in the 1930s for astute, shrewd businessmen such as Ezekiel Finkelman, and he rose to the occasion. Simultaneously, he and my grandmother (loving every minute) climbed to reach the uppermost echelons of Bogota's high society.

For me, my grandparents were my only source of warmth. They simply adored me. And I would spend the entire week longing for Friday night, when my parents and I would make our pilgrimage to my grandparents' striking three-story red brick house. The occasion was the Sabbath eve meal, which we would share as a family, followed by my special treat of being allowed to stay over and sleep at their home.

I remember the most elegant dinners there, with exquisitely beautiful dishes and settings, and the delectable tastes of Grandmother's Polish Jewish kitchen that contrasted so starkly with the spicy Colombian fare around us. Her chicken soup and gefilte fish can only be described as heavenly.

But most intensely, I remember the sensuous joy of going upstairs after dinner to sleep in their room. I would snuggle between my grandmother and grandfather in their massive European bed, enveloped by a European down comforter and huge, puffed European pillows. The freshly-starched sheets pulled tautly across the mattress were soft to the touch and carried a sweet hint of freshness.

To this day I remember the scent of my grandparents:

the strong, masculine fragrance of my grandfather's imported Old Spice cologne, and my grandmother's delicately piquant Chanel perfume.

My grandparents used to protect me. I have a suspicion that they knew what I was going through at home, and they loved me all the more – even when I turned into Debbie the Menace, which actually happened rather early in the game. I was just a toddler when I began to create havoc of major magnitude in my dear grandparents' lives.

Like the Friday night when the family was dining at my grandparents' home and I, the precocious three-year-old, was sent upstairs to bed. There, left to my own devices, I discovered my grandfather's stash of expensive imported cologne and aftershave talc. His business dealings took him from South America to Europe several times a year, and he would always return from his travels with a fresh supply of Old Spice cologne and exclusive Carven Vetiver talc powder. (After a shave, both Grandfather and Uncle Lazar would powder their faces with that most magnificent-smelling talc!)

Meanwhile, downstairs in the three-story palace, my mother was the first to notice a mysterious misty white cloud wafting down the stairs. That was thanks to innocent little me, who had dumped the contents of Grandfather's entire stock of Carven talc containers all over his bed and then gleefully jumped on the mattress!

It took the housekeepers several weeks to clean the powder out of the bed and even the closets, where it had permeated into the crevices of Grandfather's extensive wardrobe. My mother was ready to kill me.

My grandfather looked her straight in the eye and said, "Don't you touch her."

For her part, my grandmother kept her deluxe perfumes in a much safer place. But that didn't protect her from my creative (destructive) touch one night when they had just arrived home from Paris. The following morning, they were due to attend a massive, opulent wedding in Bogota. Upon her bed, my grandmother had carefully laid out the exquisite lace-accented dress that she had selected from the latest Parisian haute couture collection. It was either Givenchy or Dior, I don't remember which. And I, her four-year-old granddaughter who had been left alone in the room, delightedly took a pair of scissors and proceeded to snip the dress into pieces!

Grandmother Golda was one of the most elegant women that I have encountered in my entire life. Even the fragile black and white photos from her youth show her in splendid attire, with a cluster of pearls at her neck. Grandmother used to buy her Hermes bags before anyone knew of the brand. She had to have the very top of the line in all that she owned.

Of course, Grandmother never worked a day in her life. In Colombia of that era, high society women did not enter the workforce. She was responsible for overseeing the endless cadre of help who kept the colossal home running to perfection.

My grandparents' home was the portal to the structured aristocracy of Bogota's Jewish community. It was the venue for all the parties, luncheons and formal dinners held by the Jewish community. Personally,

I loved to wait for the doors to open every Saturday afternoon as Grandmother's lady friends would arrive for their weekly card game, a fashion event to rival any royal gathering. This parade of elderly women could have easy been mistaken for ladies heading to a cocktail party in Europe instead of going to play cards at Grandma's.

Grandfather Ezekiel and Grandmother Golda were among the most cultured people I have met in the entire world. There was not a museum they didn't visit in Europe. There was not an opera, concert, or theater anywhere in the world that they missed. Their fine sense of culture was a beacon that guides me to this day.

As I grew older, I heard Grandfather Ezekiel and Grandmother Golda described as being eccentric, stingy people. They certainly starved my mother of love, and possibly abused her as well. Yet for me, they shall forever remain the two people on earth who bestowed me with pure, unconditional love and gave me my happiest moments of childhood.

When my grandfather was gravely ill, he didn't recognize anyone – not his wife, not his children, and not the help. But when he looked at me, his first grandchild, he said, "My Debbileh, my Debbileh, my beautiful girl." And those were the last words he uttered. The hugs that he gave me, the love that he gave me, were too precious. I miss them to this day.

III

1964, Lausanne, Switzerland – Exiled

I was only an eight-year-old child. Too young to suspect the intricate plans that were being so carefully spun to break my heart.

I had just "graduated" from Grade Two. The summer sunlight glittered on the red suitcase lying across my bed. Something about its "Samsonite Red" hue matched the rouge highlights of the Impressionist painting that floated above on my royal blue bedroom wall.

I chattered away as I helped my housekeeper choose my favorite clothes and dolls (especially my newest Barbie) to pack. Father, Mother and I were about to set off on a summer vacation to faraway Europe.

I remember very little about where we travelled before we reached Lausanne, Switzerland. As Father drove the rented car into the city, I pressed my nose to the window to get a better look at the grand landscape of the Alps and Lake Geneva before me. When we stopped at a large complex of stone buildings surrounded by rustic grounds with endless trees, I thought we were going to visit a friend of the family. In any case, that's what they'd told me.

Father parked the car, and he and Mother brought me into the building. Father was carrying my red suitcase. Several nuns greeted us, but I did not understand one word they said. I spoke Spanish, not French.

I took a closer look at the sign on the building: "The Floricent Convent School."

Two nuns come out to receive us. Mother gave me to

them. And then she left. I watched the exhaust shoot out of the back of the car as she and Father drove away, never looking back.

I didn't see my parents again for two years.

***

It took over forty years till I was able to forgive my mother for sending me into exile at age eight.

Only now, I'm beginning to wonder if my father was the one who planned this scheme as a desperate way to help me escape my mother's rage and torture.

Alone in Lausanne, Alone in Bogota

I have such a phenomenal memory that I can peer back into even my toddler days with crystal clarity. But then comes the blackout: I remember virtually nothing at all from age six to eight. For whatever reason (which I shudder to consider), two years of my life have been virtually wiped out.

In a general way, I know that I began first grade at the St. George School in Bogota, a high-level British institution that my father had chosen for me. I know that I was with my grandparents over the weekends. But that's the extent of my memory from that period.

Yet I haven't forgotten a moment from age eight, the year that my parents abandoned me in Lausanne, all alone, 5,600 miles from home, at the Floricent School.

I was reduced to absolutely nothing—no family, no language, no friends, no hope. Amazingly enough, all that was left intact within me was the optimistic nature I was born with, which kicked in to save me in such very dire straits. A hug and a smile from one of the nuns might have given me the fortitude to carry on. But the odds were daunting.

The nuns took my suitcase and took me to the attic. "This is your bed and your room from now on," they told me. I was alone in this iron bed and thin mattress. The linens were a very stiff cotton, the mattress was dusty, and everything carried the musty smell of an old building.

When I peered out of the window and saw my parents driving away, I began screaming. The nun grabbed me by my hair and picked me up. As I struggled and shouted, she locked me in her iron grasp. When the nun released me, I sat on the floor in the corner of the room, hugging my legs and screaming, "Mommy, Mommy, why? Why? What did I do to you?"

The nun then put me in a closet and closed the door. "When you stop screaming, you can come out." There was no light. I was given a wastebasket in which to pee. I had no food, only water. This was my punishment, my "repentance" for the crime of screaming.

I was filled with guilt. What did I do to my parents to make them throw me away? I did enough bad things to my parents. This is my punishment. Let me die.

I crawled into a fetal position. Lying numb on the stone floor, I had no idea of whether it was day or night. I was a prisoner for three days. I tried to open the wooden door, but it was locked tight. Just a little girl confined to 14 meters, sitting in a dark room with no food, no blanket, pillow, mattress, or even a doll.

(Since that time, I remain scared of the dark. Till this day, I can't sleep in total darkness – I always open the door a peep. In my house, I sleep with open windows so I can see outside.)

When the door finally opened, I was frightened. The nuns took me upstairs and gave me my uniform, and one dressed me. But first, she totally undressed me, including my underpants, and washed me. I had no control. No power. Once I was in the uniform, she took me by the hand down the dark, wooden steps to lunch.

There were two long tables in this kitchen-like setting. All the kids were given the same food: black bread, butter and honey, and a glass of milk. I was hungry---I hadn't eaten anything for days. Food is love. This was my first experience: I'm going to stop crying. After being locked in the closet for crying, nothing was worth repeating this punishment for.

I ate the bread with all the children. We were not allowed to talk.

The next day, all the kid were served a meal. I was given only a pear. Which I refused to eat. I wouldn't eat any of the food they gave me. I went to bed hungry. By now I wanted to die. If I don't eat, I'll die faster.

For the next two days, I was given no food, just water. Then, a nun cut a pear and gave me a slice. It was sweet, delicious. I loved it! I was so surprised to experience its sweetness. This gave me ecstasy, a spiritual orgasm, the apple of the Garden of Eden. My first bite and touch of the softness of the flesh of the pear...

At night, I ate rice pudding with cherry sauce. The sweetness in my mouth went straight to my soul. I suddenly started to develop a feeling for food. I learned to take food as a comfort to ease my pain, as love for my soul. This was the first time my brain realized that food can be comforting, caring.

The next morning came breakfast – black bread with butter and honey. At lunch, I kept on eating.

I stopped crying that day. Even when my father and mother died, I didn't cry. I can't cry.

I felt guilty for being alive.......All my life.

It's a shock for a child to realize that her classmates didn't understand her. But not one child in the school talked to me. We were not allowed to interact. The nuns spoke to me in German, which I didn't understand, but that certainly motivated me to learn the language. I was taken to a classroom. To this day, I don't remember one child. I had no friends. We studied math, history, German, French, embroidery, cross point and needlepoint.

The fifteen or so nuns there did not shower (except before Sunday mass), and reeked of body odor. I was allowed to shower every day, but sometimes the water was ice cold.

I always obeyed the nuns—I was a good little girl who was certainly not rebellious. There was not one nun who was nice to me. They were all cold. They would touch me in my intimate parts. They pinched me. Maybe I've blocked this memory...

I was the only Jewish child in the entire convent school. At least I was exempt from the 6 AM Eucharist Mass and Holy Communion.

My extended family did not visit me at any point. I only found out several years ago that I was supposed to be visited by a cousin whom my grandparents sent to Switzerland for his Bar Mitzvah gift, but my mother strictly prohibited the meeting.

By age 10, I gave up on life. I'd reached the breaking point: no dreams, no future. (A normal child dreams of leaving home!) I had nothing. I felt like a robot. I didn't know at that age that suicide was a possibility. I didn't even rebel. I just gave up.

In retrospect, it's fair to admit that the nuns not only taught me to eat, but they gave me an excellent education in math, geometry, and world history. They taught me to embroider, and to approach and stand before people with confidence. Most essentially, I learned independence, knowing for a fact that I could survive on my own.

My soul was only soothed when we would go to the hills to pick cherries. Like Maria Von Trapp, I can say that the hills really were alive, with beautiful flowers and smells and snow melting from the mountains. The mountains taught me freedom. I was in a cage. Fantasy was the sky, which kept me alive. And today, over fifty years later, one of my fondest memories is that of being eight years old in the school in Switzerland, picking cherries from the graceful trees in the fields. And gaining strength.

I can still close my eyes and see myself in the cherry orchard, joyfully popping as many cherries into my mouth as a little girl could. The nuns are shouting, shrilly reprimanding me in front of everyone, and I'm so profoundly hurt.

But to this very day, I absolutely adore fresh cherries.

Ha!

***

After all these years, my heart still aches when I recall my realization of the horrible truth that Mother and Father had abandoned me. It's true that my mother had also been sent off to a Catholic boarding school by her parents, but she was a teenager at the time, not an eight-year-old child. And the convent was located in her hometown, not half a world away from home.

Two years after I was abandoned in Switzerland, my parents finally came to bring me home. I was very reserved. Inside, I tried to imagine what would happen to me now. We left the convent and returned directly to Bogota.

From that time on, I didn't want to be attached to anyone. I never knew when they would hit me or belittle me. It's a vicious circle from which I had to fight to completely disengage myself. For the better part of my life, I was physically and mentally hurt by those who should have loved me.

I never cried.

***

A Word from the Therapist

Her traumatic experiences as a youngster in the Lausanne convent brought 10-year-old Debbie to the breaking point. Her fighting spirit was exhausted, which is exactly what the convent nuns wanted. Rejected by her parents – who should have been pillars of her support – Debbie could never be happy or confident. Quite naturally, she simply gave up on happiness and closed herself up. In pain, she gave up on life.

Amazingly, Debbie's soul was not crushed. In adulthood she gathered the courage to seek help, to confront her emotions and her hurt, and to finally cry and mourn her losses. This was essential for restoring her strength and her crushed and bruised faith.

If you have personally undergone trauma at any age, you must realize that the pain is so intense that the emotional body becomes wounded to the point it can no longer deal with additional rejection. The human brain opts to shut down one's emotion so as not to experience additional disappointments from people and from life.

If you have not had proper therapy, you may be unable to identify the ramifications of the damage from a traumatic event, thus it is crucial to understand that the trauma will influence your choices in life. It is never too late to seek the path to healing and emotional self-development in order to mend the immense pain memory. With proper counseling, a great part of the traumatic experience can be remedied.

**

Back To Bogota

Returning home to Bogota, I remember that my room had been repainted. Mother continued to play cards and to go to the Women's Club. In short, life resumed as always. And so did my ruthless beatings.

The only shining light was my mother's sister Ruthy, whom I absolutely adored. I'm not sure how much Ruthy actually sensed or knew about my mother's violence, but she instinctively acted as a buffer between my mother and me whenever possible. I was like her "pseudo" child whom she loved and protected. (Ruthy herself was doomed to a terrible fate. She went into an abusive marriage to a man who loved only her money. He kept her drugged, and only by a miracle did my father find her, rescue her and bring her back to her parents' home. Yet she died childless and wasted at age thirty-seven.)

I did not return to St. George's School for Grade Five. Instead, I was enrolled in the Jewish school, Colegio

Colombo Hebreo, which had just moved to a beautiful new building in Bogota, thanks in great part to my grandfather's benevolence. I truly hated this school.

I was so terribly lost there as well. I came back from Lausanne a different person. I was this little girl, and a lot of the kids made fun of me. I became very fearful. Kids are cruel—they can smell weakness and fear in an instant. And when they do that, you become even smaller and smaller. With no reassurance from my parents, I lacked the backbone that could have given me the wherewithal to stand up to the bullies.

Recently in Miami I met one of those bullies, now a middle-aged man. I told him I couldn't ever forget how dreadfully he had treated me, but I wanted him to know now that I had been abused as a child. Tears welled up in his eyes as he clutched my hand. "I'm so sorry. I never knew," he whispered. "But Debbie, so was I. My father would beat me alive." We had so much hidden sadness in common that we hugged each other and cried. Only the two of us know this.

I should mention one memorable event from Grade Five that actually brought our class together, as the earth shook under our feet. February 9, 1967 started out routinely, but at some point during the morning I could have sworn that my desk-mate, Mark, was shaking our table. When he denied any guilt, I turned around to the boys at the desk behind us and shouted, "Are you the ones moving our table?" The second they said, "No," I screamed, "Temblor!!!!" ("Earthquake") and we all raced outside to take cover in the open, grassy fields. Then before my eyes, Ruthy, the lifesaver, suddenly ran back into the classroom to retrieve our blind classmate Mario who had been left behind in the pandemonium. Together we children held each other and actually watched the earth reel from the shock of a 7.2 magnitude quake, one of the worst of the century in Bogota.

Earthquakes aside, the Jewish school bothered me to a great extent because it was a microcosm of the stratified Colombian Jewish community. I always despised the stark religious and socioeconomic divisions. Marriage between Ashkenazi and Sephardi Jews was shunned and taboo, and rich and poor were segregated as well. Only if you had money were you welcome to the hierarchy of Colombia, and you were not allowed to mix with those who were not of means or who didn't belong to the Club or to the aristocracy of the synagogue.

In tribute to my parents, I can say that they were friends with all classes of people. Their best friends Hans and Marianne May's small house radiated warmth and love. Their daughter Debby and I have been friends throughout our lives. When my mother would go out of town for several days, I was thrilled to move in with the May's for the duration of her absence.

"We would go back and forth from each other's houses, and we've always shared the good and the bad moments," Debby May de Bettsak recalled recently. "For me, Debbie is the best! I am very proud of her achievements!"

Adjacent to my school were the gates to the absolute, ultimate opulent heart of the Bogota Jewish social and cultural scene: the Carmel Club Campestre. Its splendid grounds boasted a top-of-the-line golf course, a stunning array of advanced sports and entertainment facilities, as well as one of Bogota's most marvelous restaurants. Colombians came from far and wide to taste the renowned bouillabaisse (almost as good as my mother's), a true non-kosher delicacy dished up by the Jewish club.

Without fail, every weekend my family would flock with the rest of the Jewish community (those who could afford to join) to the Carmel Club. Here I loved to go swimming or to play golf. The adults took their pick of playing cards, tennis, golf, swimming, and so much more. But far beyond these pastimes, the Club served the indisputable role of being "the" place for Jewish Colombians to mingle and socialize.

***

My father, mother and I had one amazing passion that almost made me forget all my other problems: We travelled the world. We flew to Europe around four times a year, beginning the day before school was out for vacation when we were already aboard a flight to some of the world's magnificent destinations.

When I was a little girl and we were on vacation, my parents left me with nannies so that they could go out and dine, but if there was something special like an outdoor concert, they always took me. Soon, I was indeed old enough to fully experience the marvelous places that they travelled the earth to explore.

Our adventures brought us to the very finest museums in Europe (where we would often join one or both sets of my grandparents), and to spectacular cultural events as well. The very first opera I saw (at age seven) was a phenomenal performance of Aida in Rome, featuring Renata Tebaldi and Carlo Bergonzi. The backdrop was the ancient Roman ruins of the Terme di Caracalla, the summer home of the Rome Opera. And I'll never forget travelling with my parents to London in 1962 to see the legendary Margot Fonteyn and Rudolf Nureyev in his first performance with the Royal Ballet following his defection from Russia. We had the very best seats, sixth row center. Or in 1965, as tears flowed down my cheeks to hear the magnificent voice of Maria Callas starring in Tosca with the Royal Opera House in London, the last performance of her career.

It goes without saying that when we visited Europe, we always stayed in the best hotels. The Palace in Lucerne, the Grand Hotel. Naturally, we dined in the world's most sublime restaurants. I was already a regular at Maxim's in Paris long before it became a culinary icon.

I remember staying at the Sacher Hotel in Vienna in the early 60s. This hotel was very famous for their wiener schnitzel and for their "Sacher torte," a chocolate cake with chocolate filling and apricot preserves. Till today, the Sacher Hotel ships this cake all over the world, but I doubt that it holds the extraordinary quality I remember from those days.

I adored Madrid, which remains one of my favorite places on the globe. Just flying there for the first time was like something out of Hollywood. I was around twelve years old, and we were on the gorgeous flight from JFK to Madrid. Two of our fellow passengers in the first-class section were Richard Burton and Henry Fonda. Henry Fonda even sat next to us during the whole flight. I remember that he got drunk from too much cognac! And I'll never forget the beauty of Richard Burton's eyes.

In Madrid, we would dine in the legendary Casa Botin, which opened in 1725 and their cellar in 1590, thus said to be the world's oldest restaurant. (Hemingway said that it was also the world's best restaurant. I agreed then, but not today.) There, I tasted gazpacho for the first time, and loved to order their singular specialty of cochinillo (roast pig).

As you see, dining was always a fundamental element in our travels. My mother especially saw the world as one big kitchen waiting for her to explore. One of my most vivid memories is of joining my indefatigable mother on a trek to discover the best Italian food in Italy. This red-letter day occurred when I was around eight or nine years old.

My Aunt Ruthy invited the family to join her and her insidious husband on their honeymoon in Rome. As we landed in Rome's sprawling, green metropolis, I told my mother that I was hungry. She accepted this as being her first noble challenge upon our arrival. As my mother flagged down a passing cab, I can't forget the small smile that spread across the driver's face when she ordered him to "take us to a place where only taxi, bus and truck drivers go to eat real Italian food."

Darting in and out of a maze of thoroughfares and alleys, the driver whisked us off to a place near the train station. As we entered this rather large ristorante, we could see the madonna hard at work in the kitchen. Her husband, the host and waiter, seated us at our table. "Bring us a typical Italian meal, per favore," Mother requested.

The kitchen doors then flung open to dispatch an endless panorama of sublime food to our table. We began with the antipasti, which included various kinds of vegetables, prosciuttos, salamis, fresh figs, and Bucatini of mozzarella. And then Mother ordered the primi piatti, which was the pasta. How I remember that pasta till today! It was some type of spaghetti with Aglio oleo peroncino, which means olive oil with lots of garlic, chili peppers and finely chopped parsley, with a touch of salt and pepper. This typical Italian dish, glorious in its composition and presentation, is the first new dish that I can remember tasting. I even remember the dessert: Zuppa Inglese, a very famous Italian rum cake, along with a Tiramisu. That truck stop in Rome was the scene of the start of my love affair with Italian food.

Like every other dining adventure my mother had experienced in the most exotic places on earth, she would meticulously bring it home. After we returned from Rome, she resolutely entered her own kitchen to recreate the mouthwatering Italian meal we had eaten there. Or the wondrous fondue, my first, which we shared together in Paris. And many, many more culinary works of art that my mother discovered and mastered from kitchens dotting the globe.

Back to our travels, one of the "must" locales that Father, Mother and I never missed every summer was a journey to Austria. Father had spent his youth in

Salzburg, and his parents, my Grandfather Hermann and Grandmother Heidi, would travel from their home in Israel to join us there. I can't forget holding their hands at grand operas in the majestic halls, or visiting the country's peerless museums. They were the perfect guides to reveal to me the wonders of Salzburg, Vienna and other places that stepped out of a fairy tale.

A tale that ended in great tragedy when I was just twelve years old.

IV

1969, Bogota, Colombia – Death Strikes

"Dad, you look so tired! Come sit with me in the library," I said quietly, reaching up on my tiptoes to give my tall, handsome father a kiss as the butler opened the front door to escort him into the living room.

"Sounds good. Just give me a moment to change out of my work clothes," he told me with a smile as he slipped off his suit jacket, perfectly tailored to the last seam and button.

I was too happy for words. My mother was out with friends for the night, and I had Father to myself. Dancing across the library, I stopped just at the shelves that held the thick art history volumes teeming with world masterpieces. Tonight, I had so many questions to ask Dad – a true expert – about art.

Even before he walked into the library, I knew that Father would be wearing his silk lounging robe, newspaper in hand.

"Beethoven's Violin Concerto, it is!" he exclaimed as he entered the room. Opening the record jacket, he lifted the arm of the stereo and carefully placed its needle at the edge of the black vinyl record. The room swelled with the tones of the strings rising to a crescendo as my father settled at last in his armchair.

"What's special about Monet?" I blurted, placing a depiction of Impression, Sunrise squarely across his lap.

Slowly, lovingly, Father discussed the intricacies of the light, the brushstrokes and composition of the painting. "We'll look at the original work together when we go to the Musée Marmottan Monet in Paris," he promised. I hugged him hard, knowing that there was nothing more exciting than visiting the world's finest museums with him. There, as we would walk painting by painting through an exhibition, Father would explain each work of art to me, and even what the artist was thinking as he created the masterpiece.

When the concerto ended, Father replaced the arm of the stereo onto its stand and the record into the covers of its thin cardboard album. Mother would have never let me stay awake this late, but I had to admit I was tired and ready for bed.

"Sweet dreams!" my father said as he bent down to plant a kiss on my forehead. I fell asleep dreaming of Paris.

***

Much later that night, a loud thud woke me. The outside wall of my bedroom adjoined the garage. Sleepily, I stumbled out to the garage and lifted the door open.

I saw my father lying next to the car. I remember that my friend Jaime's father, a doctor, came to try and revive Father, but it was too late.

In retrospect, I suppose that Father had suffered a massive heart attack. Maybe he had even been trying to drive himself to the hospital before the fatal coronary plunged him into eternal darkness. Before I ever had the chance to tell my father good-bye.

I was twelve years old when my father died.

(Did he die so young of a broken heart?)

This was the shock that turned my life into a living hell. Once again I was alone, but this was the greatest alone I had ever felt.

Someone gave me a sleeping pill, and I slept so long. Then the shock struck hard. It was as if someone had stripped me of having any control over my life. That minute my safety net completely disappeared.

Father, Grandpa Hermann and Grandma Heidi

Well over forty years have passed since my father Yehudah (Jules) Finkelman's death, yet I still find myself searching for him, and for a way to pierce the cloak that still veils his past. In the Bogota of my youth, I never dared ask him or anyone any questions about the past, which was taboo. Growing up in Bogota simply meant never knowing about what had transpired in earlier times.

I do know that my father was an only child. He was born in Vienna and spent his early childhood in the wonderland of Salzburg, Austria. His parents were quite wealthy and influential people who hobnobbed with Austrian royalty at the highest echelons of society. Father lived in the lap of European luxury, and travelled the world in the giddy era of the late 1920s and early '30s. Father even took a safari to Africa with his parents, long before it entered the standard itinerary for intrepid travelers.

He was given a consummate Austrian upbringing, which meant that everything was very proper. No emotion was ever to be expressed or displayed. (As a child, I longed for a hug from my father and my grandparents who loved me dearly, yet this remained a strict taboo for the Austrian hierarchy.) But my father breathed and imbibed the culture of those seemingly enchanted times, and remained the epitome of distinctive elegance throughout his entire life. I was the eager, grateful recipient of his dazzling knowledge of culture, love of classical music and the arts, and zeal for the history of civilization. On his travels across the globe, my father even learned the art of yoga, which he taught me as a child. We used to do handstands together for twenty to thirty minutes every morning. He was my infinitely patient teacher – he even taught me how to swim – and, unlike my mother, took an interest in my schoolwork, helping me with homework. Not long before he died, he and I worked on our star project together - my school assignment to make a salt-and-flour map of Europe. Father and I sculpted a square map that covered half the table's surface and planned and executed it to perfection. We won first place in the National Science Fair!

As the winds of war had swept Austria off its golden platter, my grandparents spirited my father away on a grand escape to Palestine. (More about this soon...) In 1938, when my father was around ten years old, this pampered Austrian prince now began a new and very different life in the sundrenched, free-and-easy Mediterranean port city of Haifa.

My father was a good student, I was told. At the time of his high school graduation, Israel was in the throes of struggling for its independence from the oppressive British Mandate Authority, while facing constant skirmishes with the Arabs. Father joined the ranks of the bold "Irgun" underground army under the command of his friend Menachem Begin.

I wish I knew which covert operations my father was involved in through the "Irgun," and how he contributed to the birth of the Jewish State in 1948. Unfortunately, I never asked and was never told. But I know that my father and Begin remained friends long after they were comrades-in-arms. Even though I was only eight years old at the time, I can still recall the remarkable dinner my parents and I had with Menachem Begin and friends during a visit to New York City on November 9, 1965. That, of course, was the night of the famous blackout, and we all had to grope our way down forty-eight flights of steps from the restaurant to the street level of the pitch-black city.

Father was a tall, thin man who towered over his parents and his wife in each photo I glance at. Strikingly handsome, he epitomized elegance in his demeanor and dress, wearing his signature pristine white shirts with the most amazing ties and jackets and pants. Everything was pressed Oxford, all acquired from the finest tailors.

Following the Israeli War of Independence, I'm not sure if my father began studying or working. But I do know that around that time he was introduced to my mother via a letter. He then travelled to meet her in New York where she was pursuing her university studies in architecture, and there he proposed marriage.

My parents' wedding took place in Israel, where they set up their first household and lived for the next seven years. Recently I went to visit a very elderly couple in Haifa who had been my parents' best friends. Menachem Hakim's eyes shone when he recalled, "Their house was always open, and they were quite hospitable. We would often get together with them in the evenings. Your mother baked the most delicious cakes, the likes of which were completely unknown in Israel. Her cakes were simply out of this world!"

I was born in New York, where my parents had moved from Haifa. Very soon after my birth, they relocated for good in Bogota. There, my father joined the thriving steel import enterprise established and headed by my grandfather Ezekiel Finkelman and my great-uncle Lazar Schoenberg.

I remember the office, a beautiful place indeed. At the entrance, the imposing half-wood and half-glass doors were inscribed with the words "Finkelman and Schoenberg, Ltd." To the left was my father's office, in front of my great-uncle's office and my grandfather's office. From the time I was a small child, I loved to go there, and always felt so important! In the corporate spirit, I used to write letters on their letterhead stationery, and continue to draw and paint pictures to my heart's content.

The office was far from the house, all the way downtown. Our driver would take me directly there, and I was never allowed to wander alone in the area (strictly overprotected!).

As I've told you, all of us adored my great-uncle Lazar Schoenfeld, who was a true angel. The very first time I ever saw my father cry was when Uncle Lazar died.

Only several short months later, my beloved father would be dead as well.

An Austrian Fairy Tale Comes True

My father's father was a man of many names, and a man of great triumphs. Born "Chaim Reich" in Jagnienika (yes, the home of my mother's Finkelman family in Galicia), he was the son of Judah – "Yehudah" in Hebrew – Reich and Sima Finkelman, who was a relative of my mother's family. Judah Reich had worked as a miller in the nearby *shtetl* of Szulhanowka, and this surely brought him in close contact with the Finkelman Mills. Judah's mother Miriam was my namesake, as my full name is Miriam Devorah.

When my grandfather was only two years old in 1890, his father Judah died. Four years later, his mother Sima died as well (after burying two toddler daughters). As to the fate of my grandfather, a six-year-old orphan, I can only conjecture that he was taken in and raised by Finkelman family members.

By 1919, municipal records show that he was "Chaim Finkelman," an up-and-coming businessman living in Vienna, Austria, and engaged to marry the beautiful and talented Hedwig Wechsler of Munich, Germany. Family lore has it that they were introduced by her aunt, Tante Lotte, a *marquesa* who had married into a Christian family.

My father was born several years later in Vienna, but the family soon moved to Salzburg. By now my grandfather had morphed into "Hermann von Reich," owner of one of Europe's largest men's underwear factories, and a mover and shaker in Austrian society. Not only had he become wealthy and influential, but he held a stellar place within the exclusive coterie of personal friends of Austria's royalty and military leaders.

Photos show my grandfather vacationing with the king and queen of Austria and cavorting with members of the court in the Carlsbad resort, as well as posing with the top brass of the Austrian military in the 1920s. I'm not sure how many of these elite personas were aware of the mighty Hermann von Reich's humble Jewish Polish origins, but it is clear that he held a key position of honor.

Grandmother Hedwig, who was known as Heidi, was a tough woman, but extremely cultured. She had an amazing soprano voice. I remember her telling me that she had once been offered the role of *prima donna*, the leading female singer of the Opera of Vienna. The year was maybe 1910 or so. Yet her father squelched the proposition immediately, stating that no elegant Jewish woman would place herself in the theater and sing before an audience.

I still remember how beautifully Grandma Heidi could sing. However, I, her only grandchild, have a lousy voice. Once we sat together as we listened to the opera Aida. When I burst into singing a few bars, my grandma quickly slapped me – the only time she ever laid a hand on me. "Don't ever sing!" she admonished.

Hermann, Heidi and my father Jules von Reich took up residence in a spacious, elegant estate in Salzburg. I visited the site several times as a child with my father and my grandparents when we met in Salzburg. But as magnificent as this home was, the most intriguing magic definitely emerged from the house next door.

That adjacent estate belonged to a family quite different from the von Reich threesome. These neighbors were devout Catholics who had moved there in 1922 for the saddest of reasons. The owner, a celebrated heroic captain of the Austrian Navy, had brought his seven children to Salzburg from their native Croatia following the untimely death of their mother.

Devastated, the captain struggled to live with his own broken heart and to tend to the needs of his children, ranging in age from one to eleven. By 1926, he contacted the local abbey to request a novice nun to come work as a tutor for the children.

Maria Augusta Kutschera was thus dispatched to the von Trapp (yes!) home, and the rest is history. She and the captain were married the following year. I know for certain that my grandmother and Maria were extremely close friends.

When the Nazis annexed Austria in 1938, the two neighboring families faced a clear and present danger of the highest magnitude. The von Trapps' unconcealed disgust with the Nazi regime threatened their very existence, and ultimately compelled them to opt for an escape. The von Reichs, despite their wealth and having friends in high places, carried the stigma (and danger) of their Jewish origins. Before the noose pulled any tighter around their necks, they were left with no alternative but to flee Europe at any cost. In secret, both families spent many an hour consulting and anguishing with one another in their race against time. In the end, these neighbors resolved to set out together to escape from Salzburg, carefully trying to avoid arousing the suspicions of the ubiquitous Nazi enemies.

But to do so, they did not climb every mountain. Nor did they go anywhere near Switzerland. Instead, the real von Trapps and the von Reichs boarded a train together from Salzburg that was bound for Rome, Italy. The von Trapps told the public that they were going to America to sing (which was actually true). The von Reichs, my grandparents and father, managed to sell their assets and buy diamonds, which they painstakingly hid in the heels of Grandma Heidi's shoes. From Italy, they boarded a boat that sailed safely to the Haifa harbor.

From the moment he settled in Palestine, which would become the State of Israel ten years later in 1948, Hermann von Reich returned to being "Chaim Finkelman" until his death in 1963.

Thanks to the diamonds that Grandma Heidi smuggled out of Salzburg, my grandparents were able to buy up substantial property in Haifa. My grandmother took charge of managing the buildings, collecting the rent from tenants, and all other responsibilities involved. As my longtime friend Eli Hakim shared, "I remember how Mrs. Finkelman would visit us at our home textiles store each week to talk to us personally and take care of the needs of her tenants. The building on the prestigious Nordau Street was magnificent, and she maintained its apartments and shops quite carefully and well."

Although my grandparents barely learned to speak a word of Hebrew, they found their place within the circle of German society in Haifa, and led a quiet, satisfying life. As mentioned, my father adapted well to his new homeland, where he thrived.

Even though my grandparents missed their only son and granddaughter terribly (they never got along well with my mother), they were not prepared to ever make the trip to Colombia to visit us. They thought that Colombia was the "wild west," as my grandmother called it. It was indeed more west than Israel, I suppose. Grandmother thought that we lived in palm trees. With all the culture that she had amassed and all the people that she knew, she still thought that Colombia was a very primitive, Indian country, without realizing that it was more developed than Israel.

So instead, we used to travel from Colombia to Europe to meet them, sometimes three times a year. They would agree to fly to Switzerland; that was fine. The rest of the world was too far for them. But it was wonderful to travel through Europe with my grandparents. We went to operas at every locale and every opportunity, and steeped ourselves in culture. Each summer we always travelled together to Austria, until my grandfather died in 1963, when I was living in Lausanne. (They hadn't ever visited me there.) Then these fantastic visits stopped.

Grandma Heidi lived to the very ripe old age of 96. She was extremely cultured and very friendly. Very correct. And even in her advanced years, she remained ever so elegant.

I always loved to go to their apartment on Nordau Street in Haifa's Hadar neighborhood. It was spotless. I remember the smell, a certain aura of moth balls from naphthalene that Grandmother tucked inside the closets. Not a moth in that home!

I do recall that every (moth-free) closet was arranged to perfection. Maybe I inherited that sense of organization from her. If you come to my closets today, everything is arranged by color, by rows. The shirts are arranged by width, as are all my sweaters. Shoes are placed one shoe in, one shoe out. By colors. That I got from my grandmother.

But Grandma Heidi's iron discipline went far beyond mere closets. From the time I was a little child, I learned that everything in the house had to be structured in a very Austrian, German manner. Meaning that when she told me to put an ashtray back on the table, for example, and I didn't line it up precisely the way it had been sitting, she would give me a little slap and say "Here, not there!"

Grandmother had the most beautiful Biedermeier furniture. She had gorgeous paintings. Unfortunately, these were all stolen after she died. I don't think my grandparents really knew what they had in that house. They didn't realize how pricey Biedermeier really was. Grandmother's wardrobe alone would be worth some $300,000 today. When I came to take things out, everything was gone.

Among all that was stolen were some of Grandma's amazing collector's items. There was a book that was supposed to be for me, a 200-year-old autograph book with the signatures of all the famous people from the music and arts world such as Strauss, Bach, and all the famous composers.

When I went with my sister-in-law to clean out what little was left in Grandmother's apartment after her death, I found Grandma's underwear from the 1910s folded and pressed, stacked one on top of the other. I lifted each pair and shook it to check for any jewels that she may have stashed away inside. Then suddenly I touched something hard, and what was it? My grandfather's false teeth! We just cracked up.

Grandma Heidi had little body lotions that they used

to rub on me when I was one or two years old. And now I saw that she'd saved the bottles. I'm talking about a time when my own daughter was already born. These ancient bottles were still half full....

Looking back, I know that Grandma Heidi greatly loved me, but in true Austrian custom never showed any me affection whatsoever. In retrospect, there was indeed one rare moment when she reached out to give me a hug. I recoiled, nearly choking from the smell of mothballs that reeked from her clothing.

V

1969, Bogota, Colombia – Abused

Father is dead.

The one week of the shiva mourning period was so weird. I'm not sure if I am more in shock from Father's death or from what has been happening around me...

During the shiva, Mother and I sat on the floor, wearing only socks, not shoes. The house was packed with people – some whom I liked, some whom I didn't – coming to pay their respects. Through all the commotion, I couldn't stop thinking of my father. And wondering what would happen to me now, without him.

I'm not sure if Mother is in shock, or not. I know that she was very hurt when a very good friend of hers came up and said, "We cannot be friends anymore. Now that you're a widow, I'm afraid that you'll go after my husband."

After the week of mourning was over, we went to the cemetery to Father's freshly-dug grave. And then we came back home. My mother washed me in honey, so that my life should be sweet. I felt disgusted by her touch. She touched my vagina. Shivers went down my spine and I didn't want her to touch me again. I felt cheated by the intentions of her touch.

I've gone back to school, and "normal" life. But I can't cry.

I haven't seen my mother cry at all. She plays cards all the time – she's now captain of the Bridge competition. She goes out a lot. But. I can't talk to her. We're never allowed to talk about my father's death. Nothing. From the moment he died, she has never comforted me, or even given me a hug. True, there was barely any interaction between us in the best of times, but after my father's death, the void has become even greater.

She did take me to a psychologist. After one session I told her that that I'm never going back.

And now Grandfather Ezekiel has died. I've lost my Uncle Lazar, my father, and my grandfather within a span of several months. The three men that I loved the most on this earth. And each of them loved me so dearly.

I may be only thirteen years old, but I'm beginning to realize what life is really all about.

The Unspeakable

For as long as I can remember – and that means from my toddler days – Mother has beaten me up, pinched me, smacked me at the slightest whim, and more.

I'm eleven years old, lying down naked in my grandmother's house in Israel. I just came out of the shower. Mother called me. She raped me. Touched me all over. No caress. Didn't want to let me go. I couldn't say a word.

I was afraid.

It strangles me just to think about it. Makes me gag.

After Father died, she came into my room. Tried to touch and stroke my nipples.

I felt it was wrong. I couldn't talk about it. I was embarrassed. Afraid.

To take without asking is a rape. Abuse. Every time.

To this day, I cannot have anyone touch me.

The first time I had intercourse was to please. I was never able to enjoy intercourse. But I never considered being with a woman.

I missed out sexually. Sex = sex. Sex=love.

For me, it's a tool.

No exploring. No development. Don't touch me.

Being touched brings back memories. I couldn't let myself go into ecstasy because of the memories.

Sex for me is punishment, not enjoyment. How I would love to experience ecstasy!

Today there are workshops to develop this.

I'm afraid of it. Afraid to fall in love with love.

I fear love. I fear being loved.

Some 50 years after my father's death, my thoughts still return to those horrible moments when Mother came into my room and abused me. Yet no less painful was when she looked at me with scorn and said, "I wish you had never been born."

At Least I Have My Friends

There were exactly three saving graces to my disas-
trous teenage years: my friends Ruthy Sherman, Jaime
Demner, and Chachie (Isaac) Stern. Through it all, they
were the only people who stood by me and who made
my life livable.

The four of us were all Jewish kids in Bogota who
attended the Jewish school there, which, as mentioned,
I never liked for a minute. We all spent every weekend
at the Country Club.

Each of these three people saved my life: My dear
friend Ruthy, when she stopped my mother from
smothering me to death, and Jaime and Chachi, because
they were there for me always.

Luckily for us, our childhood was spent in an
amazingly wonderful era in Bogota's modern history
that later crashed to a violent end before our eyes.
Bogota has to be one of the world's most beautiful cities.
It's huge—around eleven million people live there. As
kids, we used to go outside all the time, visit parks, and
climb mountains. Once the security situation started
getting bad, we just visited each other, going from
house to house. We were on our own; we would go out
of the house and walk. But it was with guys and girls, so
I was never by myself. When life was unbearable for me
at home, I would pick up and go to Jaime's house. That
was only a five-minute walk. And I used to stay there
for hours. Or I'd walk to Chachi's house, and never
want to go home. Chachi stood by me always and was
like my brother. He still is, to this day.

On weekends at the Jewish club, we'd all go out for

sports of every kind imaginable. But Chachi and I didn't wait for the weekends to go to the club, which was located adjacent to our school. We had a penchant for playing golf, so every day after school Chachi and I would head straight for the green. Only after several rounds of golf would we meander home and start on our homework.

One of our favorite ventures was to go out for *empanadas*. Chachi and Jaime and I would go once or twice a week – we'd have our drivers take us, of course – to a little store near the cathedral that sold the best *empanadas*. I can still taste it today! An *empanada* is like a little pocket made of dough. I think it's made from corn. But they deep-fry it. (Just so you know, Colombian *empanadas* have nothing to do with the Argentinian delicacy by the same name.) They're crunchy, filled with meat, and absolutely delicious.

Chachi started me on a drink that we'd order together with the *empanadas*. Refajo is made of half "Colombiana," Colombian soda, and half beer. It's a cocktail that's like a shandy and 7-Up. Nothing goes better with *empanadas* than Refajo! This became my very favorite drink.

I should mention that as a child I had one more friend who lived across the street. The Mallarino family were wonderful people, and I enjoyed crazy, fun times with their daughter Sylvia. For the record, the Mallarinos were non-Jews. While I was growing up, and possibly till today, there was no anti-Semitism in Colombia.

Today Chachi Stern is a businessman living in Bangkok, and we are still in touch. Jaime Demner remained in Bogota and became a well-respected doctor. Ruthy

Sherman and I lost contact with each other for several decades, and then literally stumbled upon each other in Jerusalem. I'll soon tell you the details of our extraordinary meeting.

We Were Not Angels

In school, my friends Chachie, Jaime and Ruthy and I were all serious students. We even became friends with some of the teachers, who often went out of their way to help us. They would come to one of our houses and explain much of the material that we didn't understand in class. Our teachers were quite strict, but they prepared us very well. One thing I can say is that my group of friends never ever cheated on an exam. Nor did we ever get the answers in advance.

But, we would not exactly qualify for the prize as the most innocent students in Colombia. One trusting human being who would attest to this is our Italian chemistry teacher, Professor Lolli. We were about fifteen or sixteen years old when an extraordinary candy store had just opened in Bogota. Among their choice items were caramels that took a lot of time to chew. The day soon came that we kindly offered Professor Lolli a handful of these caramels. As he chewed them, all of his dentures fell out.

Then there was the time that some of my classmates climbed up to the top of the window frames in the classroom where they placed little transistor radios, and turned them on full blast. When the teacher came in, he searched high and low but couldn't find where the noise was coming from.

"What noise?" we students asked politely.

"But I hear noise coming from somewhere!" he insisted. "I'm going to call the principal to come here now!"

And while our teacher went off to get the principal, we quickly gathered up the radios and hid them in a briefcase, which the teacher never found.

Inspired by our success, we advanced to taking a ball of twine and wrapping it around the room like a spider web. I should mention that this was not my idea (unlike some of the other pranks we pulled).

When the teacher came in, he was shocked and shouted angrily, "Take that down now!" He went out to call the principal to come into the classroom. Once again, by the time he brought the principal to the room, we had removed the entire "web" and there was nothing at all to see.

But all this absolutely pales in comparison to our senior year, when we devised one of the world's most unforgettable schemes to take revenge. That was the year we took the long-awaited Senior Trip, and ours was to the Caribbean seaport of Santa Marta.

I won't go into details, but suffice to say that the boys in our class deserved to be punished for what they had done to us on the trip. On the last day we were in Santa Marta, it was time for the girls to take their sweet revenge.

I had about 20 pesos, while another girl had some 10 pesos. We joined forces to head to a local drug store and bought some laxatives. A very big bottle of liquid laxative, to be precise.

We returned just in time to join our class for our last meal together at the hotel. There we slipped ten pesos to the waiters and told them to pour a heaping tablespoon of laxatives into only the boys' glasses. All the girls were in on this together, and we all asked for orange juice. The boys were given some pink-colored juice which was rather tasty.

Subsequently we all went back to the hotel and then on to the airport, where we boarded our return flight to Bogota. On the plane, our friend Tania and Ruthy Sherman quickly went into one restroom and I went with another girl into the second restroom. We locked ourselves inside and laughed the whole way.

Meanwhile, the boys didn't know what to do with themselves! They were making in their pants. When the plane reached Bogota, they all ran like lightening for the airport restrooms. It was only a 50-minute flight, but still....

To this day, I don't think they knew what hit them.

My daughters are mischievous, but not as much as I was. Even they were a bit shocked when I told them this story, I must admit.

VI

1973, Bogota, Colombia –
Colombia Is Burning

The situation is becoming crazy in Colombia. The real rulers of the country are now the ruthless drug cartels, who are more evil and more powerful than any human mind can grasp.

Stakes are high in their "business." Colombian cocaine can be sold for a fabulous profit once it's smuggled to the U.S. The more coke the drug traffickers can conceal in suitcases flown into America, the more millions they make. Nothing is sacred. Any and all cruel, violent, barbaric means are fair game for the warring drug lords.

The phone rang several moments ago. It was a colleague of my mother calling from the American Embassy. As an executive and very active member of the International Women's Club, Mother is quite involved with the wives of the foreign diplomatic corps serving in Colombia. She knows them all, and is particularly good friends with the American ambassador and his wife.

"Excuse me?" she said, holding the receiver to her mouth. "Excuse me?!" she repeated, her voice rising. "This just can't be. Please tell me there's been some mistake..."

The commotion on the other end of the line was so intense that I could hear the scratching noises of screams and sirens. I've rarely seen Mother so shaken. "I'll come right away," she promised. Her hands trembled as she hung up the phone.

"Remember the American Vice-Consul?" she asked me.

Of course I did. I knew that he and his wife had only one child who was about fourteen or fifteen years old. They had been trying for many long years to conceive a second child, and finally the Consul's wife had become pregnant. We were all so thrilled to hear that she had given birth to a healthy baby girl just three days ago.

Now, when my mother repeated what she had been told in the phone call, I was too shocked to even think clearly.

"The Consul's wife was in the best maternity hospital in Bogota," Mother had told me in nearly a whisper. "Yesterday she was in her room holding her baby when suddenly a woman entered, sobbing uncontrollably."

"My sister, my sister!" the woman wailed to the Consul's wife. "My sister just gave birth to a stillborn baby. She's in terrible shock. Please, please help us!" she pleaded. "Can you please lend me your baby for only a moment to place in my sister's arms? I just know that when she cuddles the baby, this will give her the comfort and strength to begin to recover."

And the well-meaning American woman gave her the baby. Within just ten minutes – maybe less – the baby was nowhere to be found. She had completely disappeared from the hospital.

The next day at the El Dorado International Airport, a different woman appeared carrying a baby, headed for the United States. When she went to the check-in counter, she was asked to present the child's passport.

"She's just a newborn," the passenger replied. "We

haven't had a chance to apply for a passport, and I'm taking her now to live in the United States."

The woman was escorted to several different offices within the airport to tackle the red tape necessary to acquire proper travel documents. After several hours had passed, the suspicion of a flight executive had been aroused.

"I've never seen a brand-new infant so quiet," she told the mother. "Why doesn't she ever cry?"

Fumbling for an answer, the woman suddenly yanked the baby's arm like a lasso and bolted into a run. After a brief chase, the airport authorities detained the woman and seized the lifeless baby from her arms.

When they lifted the infant, they found that its body had been slashed from head to toe. All of its organs had been removed, and in their place, the body had been stuffed with cocaine. And yes, this precious baby was the daughter of the American Vice-Consul and his wife.

Mother left directly for the hospital to be at the side of the bereaved parents.

My whole body is shaking. How can a human being slaughter a newborn baby in order to use its body for smuggling cocaine? That's what drug dealing does to the morals of traffickers in Colombia. There are new, gruesome blood-chilling stories that emerge every single day.

Who will be next? How can I stay here when Colombia is going up in flames around us?

I'm calling Chachi. I don't want to be alone now.

Escape to Miami

The dark, threatening clouds over Colombia grew even more ominous as the situation worsened. Members of the Jewish community were at risk as well. We lived across the street from the Israeli ambassador, and at some point we were advised not to be surprised if certain members of the Jewish community will suddenly disappear from Colombia. The Israeli government was prepared to clandestinely fly them to Israel if they were in danger.

The teenage son of friends of our family had been kidnapped just weeks before, and his parents had given in to the kidnappers and paid millions of dollars to ransom their son. Yet they received his dismembered corpse instead.

Inevitably, I suppose, the danger crept up to touch our own door.

Mother answered the phone one evening to hear an anonymous caller say, "Senora Finkelman, your daughter's life is not safe."

Barely moments after his call abruptly clicked to an end, my mother had already hired a private plane for my escape to Miami, which was to take place the following morning. I was 17 years old.

In just a few frantic hours, I left Bogota, my home, for good.

**

When I arrived in Miami, I was completely alone.

Luggage in hand, I hailed a cab.

"Where to, Miss?" the driver asked, throwing a polite glance to his teenage passenger in the back seat.

Fishing through my purse, I found the piece of paper my mother had stuffed into my bag just a few hours earlier. (It already seemed like ages had passed since that moment.)

"5719 LaGorce Drive," I replied, trying my darndest to sound nonchalant.

In our hasty search for a place for me to live, my aunt and uncle had contacted some friends in Miami at that address who agreed to rent me a room.

On the seventh doorbell ring, my hosts finally opened the door to usher me into my first home in America. To my dismay, this was less than a momentous occasion, to say the least. The room stunk to high heaven.

I felt like a refugee. Exhausted, alone and anguished, I buried my head in the pillow and cried without taking time out to breathe. My head was bursting. What the hell am I going to do here? I didn't know anybody in Miami. I'd always been with friends, always with people, and now I had absolutely no one. I also had no idea whatsoever where to begin to turn. But I did speak English perfectly.

The only things I had were a credit card and a checkbook. That's really all I had. Which was OK, actually. The next morning, I bought a car and started exploring Miami.

It seemed logical that my first goal should be to look for a place to continue my studies. Up to just that week, I'd been studying psychology at the National University of Bogota, and I already had two years of classes under my belt. Truth is, I was only in the psychology track because my mother put me there. Her reasoning behind the decision? "Everyone studies psychology."

Earlier that year, the opportunity of a lifetime had come (and gone). My grasp of so many languages had caught the attention of a United Nations job recruiter who was visiting our university. I was actually invited to become part of the UN simultaneous translation team in the medical section, but my mother nipped that offer in the bud. "The job is in New York, and I'm not letting you go there," she declared unequivocally. "Turn around and go right back to studying psychology here in Bogota."

But here and now in the big city of Miami, it gradually struck me that those days were over. For the first time in my life, I was not being pushed into something, not being made to do something that I didn't want to do. Freedom, an entirely new concept, slowly and joyously began trickling into my brain cells.

I'd heard about Barry College, a private Catholic college near downtown Miami, and that's where I headed my sights and my new car. One glance at the campus convinced me that Barry was the place for me, and I registered on the spot for academic classes. In no time, however, I scrapped the heavy-duty subjects to follow my heart and pursue a subject I love: photography. My photography courses at Barry were a sheer delight. To this day I love taking pictures, especially of flowers, people, and landscape scenes.

Meanwhile, back at the home on LaGorce Drive, the scene was not a very pretty one at all. With every passing day, it was getting harder and harder to breathe over the stench in my room. One day I opened a window to get some fresh air. In a shot, the landlady darted in and slammed it shut!

The next day I opened the window, and the same scenario repeated itself. Fortunately, the landlords left for vacation soon afterwards. I wasted no time in calling someone to come over and help me look for the source of the putrid, sickening odor that permeated the house. We began a thorough search of the house, ending with a climb up to the attic. There we were greeted by a nest of hundreds of rats!

I certainly didn't wait for my landlords to return for me to say good-bye to them. I just stuffed my things into the car and floored the accelerator to get me out of this hell hole. I called my mom to tell her about the rats and about my decision to leave without further ado. That very day, I rented my first apartment in Miami.

That night, I simply couldn't shower myself enough. I washed and washed my clothes and I washed myself again and again. I seem to recall that I even dipped into the ocean to immerse my body. Then I went for a swim in the pool just to keep washing and cleansing my body and soul, ridding myself of the disgusting way that these people lived.

I never saw my landlords again. But being a very well-mannered person, I did send them flowers and a note that said, "Thank you for everything, Debbie Finkelman."

I did do that.

Despite the existing danger reigning in Colombia, my mother and grandmother remained in Bogota. From what I understand, they never received direct threats to their lives, although the environment was unstable and quite volatile. Maybe it was my mother's social life that kept here there. I never really asked her.

Most important, when I first moved to Miami, Mother didn't come to visit me at all. That was the biggest favor she could bestow upon me. So, this became a good time in life for me. I learned about myself. And started wondering what would become of me.

My soul was not free, but my mind and body certainly were. I was on my own. I could do whatever I pleased. True, I had to learn to survive, meet people, take care of myself, and take command of my life. But as daunting as those tasks might be, they were far less frightening than the prospect of going back to Bogota, a terrible thought indeed. Drug wars aside, I couldn't face the thought of returning to a society with such a giant, cruel socioeconomic gap, which I hated with a passion, and still hate to this day.

Miami was wonderful.

In truth, I've always loved Miami since I was a little girl. Only a two-and-a-half-hour plane ride away from Bogota, Miami was a perfect get-away spot for vacations, often with other family and friends. I remember spending many a summer break there with Chachi and his family in particular.

I've seen Miami go up and down and now up again. When I was growing up, it was a magnificent city. I have vivid memories of going to Lincoln Road while on vacation, a beautiful place to see the water. In my mind, it was a combination of verdant green and cerulean blue. I always loved how we could walk freely in the streets.

For many of my birthday celebrations as a child, we used to go to Miami to a restaurant called "Famous," which served Jewish food. We would all be there: my grandparents, my parents and me, and my mother's brother and his wife and their kids. I used to love that restaurant so much!

Then Miami started to decline. You could see it most clearly when you went to Miami Beach on the Ocean Drive. There were little hotels donned in beautiful Art-Deco décor, but on their balconies you would see elderly people sitting on chairs waiting to die. Until a movement began to reawaken the city to become the Art-Deco capital of the States, to make Miami young again.

I was living in Miami at the time the revival started, sparked when a famous eatery was completely transformed into becoming a modern restaurant and a recognized art-deco gem.

There was also the first good Italian restaurant in Miami, the "Mezanotte." The atmosphere was young and vibrant, with music pounding with such intense rhythm that people would stand on the tables and dance. I watched the whole city change. The TV show *Miami Vice* also helped, and attracted the young crowd to flock to Miami's beaches and homes.

Colombian Jews only began moving to Miami when things started getting bad in Colombia. Indeed, my mother was one of the first to buy an apartment in Miami around 1978-1979. (She later gave it to us as a wedding gift.) Afterwards everyone we knew started buying up apartments in Miami.

So, in 1975 I found myself living in Miami and I felt at home. It was a nice time in my life. I was in La-La-Land. I was happy being by myself, and happy to be going out. Happy that I didn't have to come home to somebody who was always putting me down or beating me up.

In a way I was free of my mother, but a part of me was always afraid that she would suddenly show up in Miami. Nevertheless, I was happy. I was able to wake up and watch the sunrise, go out for a walk at night, and do whatever I wanted without somebody telling me, "No, no, no." The two things I hate the most are the words "no" and "don't." Till this day.

Then one day, my mother comes to Miami! And this leads to how I met my husband.

PART 2:
Travels to the Summit

VII

1977, Miami, Florida – A Very Special Guest

I wonder what he looks like....

I've only spoken to this man once over the phone, but I like his voice, especially his Israeli-accented English. He's thirteen years older than I am, and he's already accomplished so much in his life. I guess I've accomplished quite a bit myself, come to think of it, but not in the same way....

It's true that I haven't yet laid eyes on him, but we did have a great conversation yesterday. So great that I invited him to join me and my mother for a Rosh Hashanah (Jewish New Year) dinner tonight at our house, and he accepted on the spot!

Mother started cooking with a passion the second I mentioned that we are having a special guest. She's hard at work preparing her famous chicken soup. And homemade gefilte fish, of course. I've made an amazing paella, but without seafood, and I'm doing the rice. I had the best time this morning baking a big chocolate cake for dessert.

I hope he'll like what I'm wearing. It took me some time to choose just what would be best for the occasion. But I must admit that if the mirror doesn't lie, I feel proud how irresistible I look at this minute in my blue skirt, white chemise top, and my favorite earrings.

That's him at the door now!

***

And behind that door stood one very, very handsome man, dressed impeccably in khaki pants, a white turtleneck and a natural camel-colored suede coat.

Time for dinner. Time for a New Year to dawn. Time for us.

Love & Marriage

Mother made her way to Miami at the beginning of August, 1977, just when I least expected her. By this time, I had rented a cozy apartment and had a nice roommate. We were just having a good old time, and my mother suddenly appeared at the doorstep.

But the plot thickens. Not long afterwards, my mother's cousin from Israel, came to visit and stay with us for three days. I had no idea at the time that this was not an innocent visit. Instead, he was in cahoots with my mother to cook up a divine plan.

"Listen Debbie," he told me, looking straight into my eyes. "You are the only living relative of your Grandmother Heidi in Israel. You absolutely must visit her, and soon. She is not doing well. She's an older woman who is ailing." Grasping my hands, he repeated solemnly, "You are the only living descendant that she has."

Later that night, I'd come to a reconciliation of sorts. "OK, Mommy, I'll do it. I'll travel to Israel to visit Grandmother. But - only if I can stop in London on the way back to see some plays and visit a few museums."

Mother didn't bat an eyelash when she answered, "OK. Fine. You'll leave tomorrow."

So, the next day I was already packed and en route to visit my grandmother. Reaching the Haifa seaport city at last, I opened the door to Grandmother's elegant apartment, my hands shaking as my cousin's words of doom echoed in my head.

I never saw my grandmother as healthy and alive as she was then. I had the most amazing stay with her. We walked and we talked and we laughed. She regaled me with stories from her past, like how she'd nearly been a prima donna opera singer and how beautiful her life had been. In those few days that I was in Israel, Grandmother filled me in on her extraordinary history.

And then my very good friend Orna came to Grandmother's home to visit me. Orna and I have been friends since we were kids, and her parents were my parents' best friends.

"Come have dinner with us, Debbie!" Orna exclaimed. "My brother Eli will be there too!" Looking back, I see how they had everything planned. All this was to lay the groundwork for The Goal: to make the *shidduch*, the matchmaking set-up.

Dinner was delightful. I loved being with the Hakims, and seeing Eli was a special treat. Somewhere near the time that dessert was being served, Eli sat down next to me and said, "I have a friend who is in Miami that I'd like to introduce you to. Can I ask you a favor? His brother is here in Israel and I would like you to meet him."

"OK, great," I said with a smile, reaching for the coffee cake that Margot Hakim was heaping on my plate.

The last day I was in Israel, I arranged to meet my future husband's brother Doron in Tel Aviv. I couldn't believe what a gorgeous man he was. I figured that his brother must be handsome as well.

"Could you possibly do me a favor and take a shirt back to Miami to give to my brother?" Doron asked me politely.

"Sure. Absolutely," I declared.

Everything was already prepared. So, the package that I was given to deliver contained a men's shirt manufactured by HOM of France. (Which happened to become our first business together.)

When I got back to Miami, I dialed my future husband's number. To my surprise, a woman's voice answered, "M...... Residence."

"Oh boy," I thought. "He must be very wealthy or married or something." I didn't understand, because in Colombia we didn't have telephone answering services. So I left a message, and he called me back.

This led to our next phone calls and my invitation to him to join me and my mother for a Rosh Hashanah New Year's dinner.

To this day I don't know if he fell in love with me or my cooking. But the next day he asked me out. This was September 1977. Six months later we became engaged, and we were married on July 9, 1978.

The Wedding

To this day, 40 years later, people are still talking about our elegant, magnificent wedding.

My mother had gone back to Colombia beforehand, so I made all the arrangements on my own. But I guess I inherited her expertise for this kind of assignment, thank goodness. This became the first of the many grand affairs I have since made.

The wedding was held in Miami at the Eden Rock Hotel, which was owned by family friends. The ceremony took place in the Rotunda Room, a luxurious circular room with wood-paneled walls and Louis I chairs.

The officiating rabbi, who was from the beautiful Beth David Synagogue, took his place beneath the *chuppah*, the traditional bridal canopy. Little angel figures brimming with flowers lined the path to the canopy, a tiered-lace splendor draped with turquoise and pink roses.

Suddenly, all eyes turned towards the massive doors in the distance. My heart started pounding. I felt exhilarated. I'm finally getting married to the man of my dreams! As I saw him standing in his tuxedo waiting for me, a smile covered my face.

At precisely 6:05 PM (I'd called the wedding for 6:00), the doors opened. The groom entered first, escorted by his brother. His father followed, arm-in-arm with his daughter. My uncle then walked me down the aisle, alongside my mother. How both of us missed our deceased parent being with us at that moment!

Just after we were pronounced man and wife, I cannot forget the next moment: My mother did not congratulate me. Instead, she said with brutal frankness, "No refunds, no returns."

I felt so hurt, not knowing if she was attempting humor or being honest. Till today, I don't know if she was happier to get rid of me or I was happier to get rid of her....

Following the ceremony, our guests were feted with cocktails served in two gorgeous locations: indoors by the poolside, and outdoors overlooking the ocean. The cocktail menu: shrimp, lobsters and the most amazing cocktails, liquor and wine, which flowed freely for all.

Afterwards, the guests were ushered into the elaborate banquet room for the main meal. Pink and white tablecloths were graced with the most magnificent china and the most beautiful glassware for red wine, white wine, champagne and water.

I worked closely with the florist to create unforgettably gorgeous and very unusual centerpieces fashioned from four tall cubes of Lucite. A cascade of pink, turquoise and white flowers was arranged at the base of each cube, combining roses, tulips and more. Since the cubes were transparent, you could easily see and talk to the people sitting across from you on all sides of the table.

I made sure that the dinner was "French-served," not a buffet. (I don't believe in buffets.) Served from the right, picked up from the left. Every single dish had the wine I paired to it. I was only twenty-one years old, but I already knew how to pair white wine to fish.

The menu opened with vichyssoise, a cold potato soup. Then, perhaps for the first time at an American wedding, a Caesar salad was served in a cocktail glass (I introduced this European-style presentation), followed by a small glass of sorbet, to cleanse the palate. Chardonnay wine was the choice vintage for this portion of the meal.

Then came the main course: filet mignon with mushroom sauce served over potatoes Anna and asparagus tied with little miniature carrots. I remember it like yesterday!

At the proper time, the lights were dimmed to signal the arrival of the desserts. The waiters made a dramatic entrance carrying flaming baked Alaska, very much in style then. The *piece de resistance* was a most magnificent Viennese table that I created.

Our wedding cake was five feet tall. We saved the top layer to cut for our first anniversary.

When I first began planning the wedding, the initial guest list totaled 1400 people from both sides. And I said, "Over my dead body will I have a big wedding!" To avoid that scenario, I made certain to hold the wedding in Miami. Friends in Bogota had offered to host our wedding, but I politely declined. However, I made sure our wedding was scheduled for July 9th, when school was just getting out in Colombia, so not everyone could reach far-away Miami. In the end, only our closest friends attended. These guests, numbering exactly 189, came from Israel, Switzerland, Canada, Colombia, and the world over.

The funny thing was that I got a lot of criticism from the Colombian guests, because this was the first time that any Colombian had seen place cards at a wedding. And I had everything so extremely organized. They said to me, "How dare you put me sitting next to these people!" Here everything was organized, everyone had a table to sit at. In Colombia, a thousand people come to an event and scramble for seating. Not my style.

The music was just outstanding. Joe Israel and his quartet performed, featuring our talented friend Marian Rosenberg at the piano. My husband made the musical arrangements. His own love affair with music had begun at age five when he took his first piano lessons. He later studied at the Conservatory of Music until he finished his military service, and to this day is an avid music lover and talented pianist.

Our wedding started near 6:00 PM and ended at 2:30

AM. And I was the one who closed the doors. I didn't want to miss one minute of my wedding, just to enjoy it!

I can honestly say that this was one of the most elegant weddings I've ever attended. Not just because it was my own.

A Dream Honeymoon & a Great Bargain

The next day we set off on our honeymoon.

My husband was very close to Ted and Lin Arison, owners of the Carnival Cruise Lines. Their wedding gift to us was an island cruise honeymoon aboard their private cabin in the Carnival, their second ship.

In addition to enjoying the fabulous cruise, our honeymoon sparked my love for beautiful dishes. In the States, it is standard procedure for a new bride to register at a particular shop for her china, silver, glassware, etc. The Bridal Registry, evidently an American invention, enables you to select the exact pattern and wares that you want your guests to buy for you as gifts. I registered for baccarat glasses, gold flatware, and very nice china dishes, and received the full list.

Before my wedding I had gone back for a visit to Colombia, and my aunt threw a bridal shower in my honor. The one request that I made to my friends and family was not to give me a thousand gifts, but just to get together, pool their funds and give me something that I could take to the United States that would last forever. So, they collectively gave me the most beautiful sterling silver bowls. Till today, these hold an honored place at the center of my table.

On the honeymoon cruise, our Love Boat sailed through San Juan, Puerto Rico; St. Thomas; and St.

John's. At St. Thomas, the Carnival docked and we took off to stroll across the lovely island. I remember the moment like it was today. At a particular corner store in the quaint town's center, my husband and I saw the most beautiful black and white set of china in the shop's window. I said, "Sweetheart, let's buy it!"

I recall the saleswoman calling our attention to the fact that this set was a service for twelve. But there was a problem, she noted seriously. There were no soup bowls and no soup tureens, so the set had been marked down significantly.

We bought it. I think we paid around $50 per place setting, and I'm talking about over 40 years ago. I told my husband that we should buy it, bring it aboard the ship and then we could use it at home in the future. As for the missing items, I assured him that we could always buy the remainder of the dishes in Miami, no problem.

Back at our new home in Miami, I lovingly put away each piece of the beautiful china set. And whenever I was out shopping, I'd start looking for replacement pieces. My mother and I both looked wherever we could, even extending the search to Macys and to Fortunoff in New York. But we didn't find anything in either Miami or New York. We went to every store possible, and nobody, but nobody carried this pattern of china.

Exactly one year to the day after we returned from our honeymoon, we took my mother, her cousin and daughter for a drive up to Palm Beach. As we passed a store on Worth Avenue that sells the very finest china in the world, I shouted, "Mommy, there they are! Those are my dishes!"

Excitedly, we entered the store en masse, and I told the woman manager of the shop that I had this exact set and needed some missing pieces.

"That can't be true," the manager responded evenly. "You can't own that set."

"But I do," I almost shouted. "Those are my dishes! I bought them on my honeymoon a year ago when we were in St. Thomas."

"So, you're the one," she exclaimed. "All of us in the business know about you." I listened dumbfounded as she continued, "Princess Margaret of England had a residence on the island of Antigua, and she was getting rid of the china. The local china shop, however, had made the mistake of omitting one important zero to the price tag."

And I bought that china. Here in this shop in Palm Beach thirty-seven years ago, the price tag on one soup tureen was $1200. Each place setting cost about a thousand dollars. Today the set is one of the china services that I have in Miami and use with delight.

And that was my big bargain of a buy on my honeymoon.

VIII

1983, Miami, Florida – Motherhood's Mysteries

Even though she's only eighteen months old, my little daughter knows that there's something special in the air. She's just watched her three-year-old sister skip happily out the door, hand in hand with her father, on their walk to the park to gather pinecones for our Thanksgiving table.

The turkey has been roasting for hours, and I can hear the pan juices sizzling. It's already time to baste it again! I bend down to pull open the heavy oven door and lift the golden turkey out to place it on the counter. But where is the turkey baster that I just had one minute ago?

At that moment, my daughter's piercing scream cuts through my heart. "What happened, sweetheart?" I shout as I spin around to look for her. And there's my precious baby standing next to the oven door that I'd left open for just a split second. Her face contorted with pain, she lifts her little hand to show me the seething, blistering burn.

I felt devastated and guilty that I had unintentionally hurt her. Looking back, I'm not sure which of us suffered more, my daughter or me. But to this day, the strangest part of this story is the light pink scar that remains on my daughter's right hand. My husband has a light pink scar in the identical place on his right hand from a childhood accident he's long forgotten.

The mysteries that bind our children's lives to our own lie just beyond any explanation that I pretend to grasp.

Career Woman, Wife & Mother

After my future husband had been discharged from the Navy at age twenty-one, he headed for the United States where his relative Meshulam Riklis advised him to study at his own alma mater, Ohio State University Business School. Following graduation (Cum Laude), he began working for Riklis, who at the time was like the Bill Gates of retailing in the U.S. Once we were married, my husband was ripe and ready to launch into the business world on his own. He just needed the right opportunity at the right time. And his business acumen was sharp enough to realize that the United States market was ideally suited for the import of the HOM line.

HOM was based in France, and my husband didn't know a word of French. We didn't miss a beat as I stepped in as the translator, and before long, he and I were designated as the exclusive US distributors for this chic men's clothing designer label. Thank God for my love of languages!

Our success with HOM spurred my husband to expand the business into the realm of women's clothing as well. We grew to open a company that served as the sole distributors for Gideon Oberson swimwear to the United States, Central and South America, all the way to Argentina. Within a matter of a few short years, we became the second largest distributors of women's swimwear in the entire United States.

My unofficial position increased beyond "translator" to the executive post of Public Relations Director and head of the fashion shows. I was the one who brought the buyers to view our shows. But I remained the translator, especially where businesspeople from South America were involved.

Even though we had a cadre of reps, my husband and I travelled a lot. We would go to the warehouses, some Spanish-speaking, and to the shows. We travelled frequently to New York and to Dallas.

He and I worked well together. He dealt with the finance and commerce, and I loved my work as translator and fashion show coordinator

In truth, my husband brought his skilled business sense and experience to our enterprise. I had no background whatsoever in the wide world of commerce. But I had no choice. I learned it! That's the one thing I made myself do. Never fall down, always stand proud. And never be afraid to learn more.

Now the Mother Is Me

Did I mention that my mother moved in with us newlyweds? Soon after we were married, the situation in Bogota became too horrific for everyone. She made the quick decision to flee, and sold or gave away everything there to come live with us in Miami. More details to follow about that cozy arrangement, but you can believe me when I say that it wasn't easy.

Yet the moment I became a mother when my first daughter was born, my whole life changed. It was a new adventure. I saw this little baby cradled in my arms, and I swore that from this child on, all my children would have only love. There would never be pain. I would not let them be hurt by anyone. This changed my life for the better.

My second daughter was born a year later, and I looked forward to waking up every morning and smelling my babies' morning breath. To watch them smile whenever they saw me. I placed their cribs next to my bed. I needed to have a sense of belonging.

What was amazing is how my mother changed. With the girls, she was a completely different woman. I could see her eyes light up when she held them in her arms.

Then there was my husband, who had married at age 35 and become a father at age 37 when our first daughter was born. He was in a state of awe when he held his child. And that man just loved to come home. There wasn't a day that he didn't come home from work and take the girls for a walk on the beach, collecting seashells along the way, swimming with them, playing with them in the pool. Always.

In my children I found the friends I adored, the laughter I so loved at the funny things that they did. I used to sit for hours on the floor and play with them.

It was fun. For my daughter's first birthday, I ordered a cake the size of a table in the shape of a huge bunny. Everyone came, and we all had babies. I made her that birthday cake. I made all my children's birthday cakes, including one that was a carousel with horses around it.

My oldest had a favorite Strawberry Shortcake doll that I still keep, along with a "My Little Pony" that belonged to her little sister, whose toys I have till today. I took my daughters across the U.S. and the world for sightseeing, swimming, snorkeling and dining together. Every trip was a new adventure for me. Travelling with my children gave me a sense of happiness and belonging as I showed them the world. It also enabled me to continue the introduction to culture that I had received as a child. I couldn't have been prouder of how the girls absorbed all I tried to teach them from the world over. When my mother moved to Israel, I used to bring them to visit her every summer, every winter and sometimes in between. We would come for two-month stretches, filled with visits to the beach, the park, and nature walks. Both girls absolutely love nature.

There was nothing that they wanted that I didn't get for them. But at the same time, as my daughters were growing up, I taught them the value of the dollar, and the need to earn what they want in order to gain the self-respect that is needed in life. From the age of sixteen, both girls worked.

My daughters are the kindest, warmest human beings and true friends. They will fight for their own friends, tooth and nail. I'm very proud of what they've achieved. I'm very proud of the women that they have become. I'm very proud of my motherhood. Looking back, I have no idea how I was able to be a good mother to my children. I never, ever raised a hand to them.

Dogs Are Our Best Friends

I've loved dogs all my life. From the moment I opened my eyes as an infant, our Doberman Pinscher "Tony" was there. He wouldn't let anyone come close to my crib.

The second dog of my life was my father's boxer, who was also named Tony. That dog was magnificent. Yet he was soon exiled from the Finkelman home for perpetrating an unspeakable crime: at one of my mother's meticulously planned and orchestrated dinner parties, Tony made a grand entrance, deposited some poop in the dining room and then helped himself to something to eat from the table. My mother's ultimatum to my father was, "Either the dog or me." I don't know what they did to Tony, actually...

When my father died, I went into such shock that my mother decided to get me a little black poodle. "Cookie" was the love of my life. She slept with me and went everywhere with me. I don't know what happened to her after I left for America. I simply couldn't take her with me. I felt such emptiness without her, and guilty for not being able to bring her to me.

My husband grew up in a home without animals, so for the first years of our marriage we didn't have a dog around the house. Then, unexpectedly, during a visit with the girls to my mother in Israel, I caught sight of an adorable miniature jet-black poodle with one streak of white, which was sitting in the window of a pet shop opposite my mother's apartment. I told the girls, "Let's buy this dog, and we'll keep her here. Don't worry. I'll deal with Daddy." Over our two-month stay, she became the most spectacular, smartest dog I've ever encountered. When I would go buy her those little dog candies and I would ask her, "Do you want some chocolate?" She would answer, "Yum-yum!" She was amazing. She used to sit like a princess, a true diva.

On our return home, I casually mentioned to my husband, "By the way, I bought my mother a dog. (I lied to him.) When she comes for a visit, she'll bring the dog, Snappy, here with her, because she's by herself." My mother brought the poodle to Miami. And who falls in love with her? My husband. This poodle used to sleep between his legs.

I love travelling with my children, and took the girls with me to Paris when they were around twelve or thirteen. I love to walk, clocking many miles a day, and the girls were just as happy to stride alongside. That trip, I took our little French poodle with us to Paris. Of course, we couldn't bring Snappy into museums, so I switched off, leaving one daughter outside in the garden with the dog and taking the other one into the museum.

The beautiful thing was that dogs are so loved by the French that in every restaurant we frequented, the dog was seated next to us. The chefs made steak tatare for her! She was this little prima donna in the top restaurants in Paris, partaking of the finest meals. La Coupole, Chez Andre—all the renowned eateries. And because it was the summer and quite hot, we had to carry Snappy from place to place. This little French poodle in Paris.

I bought another dog and today we have two Malteses, aged twelve and thirteen years old, whom we love dearly. I cannot go to sleep without touching the little one. Dogs add love and peace to my life. I look at their eyes and their souls, and when I hug them I'm filled with a certain sense of peace. The innocence that I see in the eyes of every animal gives me something so inexplicably beautiful. These animals simply give unconditional love. They fulfill my soul.

I love cats, but I'm very allergic. Except to my older daughter's cat.

It doesn't matter what animal you keep for a pet,

because you're a human being with a soul. But there's a huge difference between people who hate animals. How can someone hate something they don't know, something that will give such intense love? I can understand if someone's afraid, perhaps. But I can't understand how anyone could hate an animal.

I wish I could explain to you how these beautiful souls of animals became part of my healing process. I felt peace as I held them.

People Who Opened My World

In Miami, we had the most wonderful international circle of friends. To this day, I owe these friends a lot. In particular, the Barbar family, George and Alice, her mother and their four children. These remarkable, prominent people are Christian Arabs who left their native Beirut for Jamaica and eventually settled in Boca Raton, Florida.

We used to visit them in Boca and enjoyed great adventures together on their huge yacht, the *Lady Alice*. George is the one who introduced me to the brother of the King of Saudi Arabia and the actual King of Morocco. Alice is the one who introduced me to the magical world of Lebanese Arab cuisine.

Alice cooked beautifully. She showed me the intricacies of making yogurt, *labeneh*, by adding a little "old" yogurt to milk, cooking it and letting it boil for three minutes. Cool, bring to a second boil, and strain the liquid through a gauze cloth. Let it sit overnight, and you end up with simply delicious yogurt. Alice also taught me how to make the very best tabbouleh. She used a lot of parsley, cucumbers and scallions and a small amount of bulgur. The dressing? Loads of lemon juice, a little bit of olive oil. And there was also Alice's outstanding *kibenaya,* made of mincemeat and bulgur topped with tahini, baked in the shape of diamonds and served warm. Delectable!

Thirty years ago, my dear friends and Miami neighbor Dina Gershoni, who is Moroccan-born, and her sister-in-law Rivka Eliani from Uzbekistan, were the women who opened my senses to the fabulous world of Moroccan food, which they get full credit for teaching me to love and cook. Actually, theirs is not a "typical" Moroccan style, but a blend of influences from Syria, Iraq, Turkey, Italy, France and Spain. I think that as Marco Polo traversed the Silk Route, he brought a bevy of spices to Morocco. Dina and Rivka brought these most colorful, tasty spices of the world to my own kitchen. They had both mastered the art of Moroccan cooking at its finest. One of their delicacies is Moroccan Fish, a fabulous, very different combination of fish and vegetables, which I love to eat with rice.

The Chutzpah to Go Out & Conquer the World

When I hit the fearsome age of forty, I took a leap of independence (or "chutzpah," if you will) that brought me to the wilds of Japan on a mission of mercy. Even my husband was shocked when I made this bold move.

The instigator was my amazing friend and role model Diane Cummins, of Columbus, Ohio. Diane was one of the most talented hostesses and chefs I'd ever encountered. Her reputation grew to the point where the company she headed was selected to cater the official parties and dinners for the governor of Ohio. From catering to flowers, Diane taught me so much, and like my mother, she too was a master of the art of protocol.

Diane inspired me to join her in an important endeavor that she had personally dreamed up, breathed life into, and implemented. This creation, called "Operation ALY" (America Loves You), was aimed to show appreciation to American military troops serving throughout the world. Diane would travel to US bases in faraway places across the globe to bring some joy to the American soldiers, treating them to traditional food, drinks and gifts donated by the people of the United States. When she invited me to join her on a trip to American bases in Japan and the demilitarized zone in Korea, I was thrilled to accept.

Then I broke the news to my husband that I was going. He said no. I retorted that my expenses were being covered, the trip would not cost him one cent, and that I was off to Japan, period. (Ha! Independence!)

The day before I left, I don't know why, but a feeling came over me that I was onto something very special. As my own contribution to "Operation ALY," I went to my children's school, told the principal where I was headed and why, and asked if the schoolchildren could please write personal letters to deliver to the US troops in Japan. The principal loved the idea, and we went from class to class. Every child wrote to a soldier, along the lines of: "Dear Soldier, My name is Lisa. My name is William. I am in 5th grade. How are you? I love you." I carried the precious box of "Dear Soldier" letters with me on the plane.

I'll never forget coming to the first base, and I asked

the soldiers, "Would you like a letter from a child in the US?" They came by the hundreds to ask, "Do you mind if I take another letter? I haven't heard from my own family. Do you mind if I write back to this little girl?" There were times when I had to hold back my tears as I gave out the envelopes. Happily, this "Dear Soldier" letter project that I personally started grew to become an integral part of Operation ALY's important, loving work. It's still carried out by schools today.

That wonderful trip to Japan and to the demilitarized zone perpetrated the sense of being able to give of myself to others for their wellbeing, and fulfilled my life with purpose. This became an enlightening turning point in my life. At that moment, I realized that I'm not only a wife and mother, but a woman who can be kind to other human beings. Beyond the sights I saw and the things that I did, this trip also marked the point when nobody or nothing could hold me back.

In time, I accelerated my involvement in voluntary community service, becoming very involved in Children's Variety, the American Cancer Association, the Alzheimer's Association, the Parkinson's Disease Foundation and the City of Hope Hospital. The City of Hope, one of the top hospitals in the world for cancer and AIDS research, caught my heart after I took a tour there and grasped the magnitude of their lifesaving work. Back in Miami, I arranged their fashion show gala (my forte, after all), and was always quite hands-on in making these and other fundraising activities a success. When Miss Universe and Miss USA came to Miami on behalf of the hospital, we held private parties for them. For doing my part, I was honored as the City of Hope Hospital's "Woman of the Year."

Of course, community service comes to me straight from my DNA. As I mentioned, my grandmother Golda was the founder of WIZO (Women's International Zionist Organization) Colombia, and my mother later took over its leadership. To her credit, my mother was also very involved with the National Women's Club and the Bogota Garden Club, and one thing she taught me is that it is always good to pay back. One of the first things that I did when I reached Miami was to help found the first WIZO chapter in Florida, which thrives till this day along with eight other chapters that have since been founded.

Today, I champion humanitarian efforts that are especially close to my heart. To ease the pain of disadvantaged youth, I am now encouraging exciting projects to groom these young men and women for top careers in the culinary world, to give them hope that their lives can improve. This has become my single-minded drive.

My latest venture is the most exciting of all. The newly-established Debbie Matzkin Foundation will offer scholarships for needy youth to learn the culinary trade. One main project is in cooperation with La Confrérie de la Chaîne des Rôtisseurs, the renowned French international gastronomic society which recently named me as a "Grande Dame." Beginning with their new initiative, a Cooking School in Tel Aviv for underprivileged youth (the very first La Chaîne school outside of France!) taught by international master chefs, I will sponsor a number of the youthful participants. This is my gift towards a better future for these young people and for us all as well.

Through charity work, I've learned to give wholeheartedly and to encourage others to give as well. My rewards have been greater than I can fathom.

VIII

Haunted

The party is dazzling, the food is perfect, and my guests are enjoying every minute. "Debbie, you're a wonder!" my friend exclaims, planting a kiss on my forehead. "You absolutely must tell me your secret for making these hors d'oeuvres. They're fabulous!"

"You'll never believe how simple they are to prepare," I tell her, as I smile at the crowd of guests devouring the food with gusto. "All you need is..."

A loud, thunderous crash suddenly shakes the room. Hors d'oeuvres and shattering glass go flying as the main serving tray is flung to the floor with a vengeance. My beautiful living room suddenly looks like a battlefield.

"Debbie, you are such a horrible failure!" rings out my mother's shrill voice. With both hands, she hurls each lavish serving dish onto the floor. "You've never done one thing to be proud of. You're worthless! GET OUT OF THIS HOUSE NOW!"

I want to die of humiliation. I race out of the house, but my mother is chasing me. She throws me to the ground and punches every part of my writhing body. I recognize that look of murder darkening her eyes. Her hands reach for my neck. "Stop, Mommy, please stop! You're hurting me so much!"

I wake up moaning. Another nightmare. Every night, every night. My mother has been dead for a decade, but I have no peace. She haunts me at every turn.

She's still controlling my life.

Releasing My Mother, Regaining My Soul

And so it was that not long after we were married, my mother moved in with me and my husband to our apartment in Miami. I should blame Pablo Escobar, the vicious Colombian drug lord, for mercilessly destroying the society and leaving my mother no choice but to flee Bogota for her life. But somehow, she brought her own reign of terror straight into our newlywed nest.

From Day One, my mother started criticizing and finding fault with me, reaching a climax by shouting her mantra, "I wish you had never been born!" I came crying to my husband, and he confronted her squarely.

"Anita, why did you say that?"

"I didn't say anything," she shot back, with a perfectly straight face.

My mother was always a liar. Yet her lying rose to the pathological level when she suffered a head injury and cerebral blood clot in an accident soon after my father died. Essentially, she could not differentiate between truth and lies. In consequence, she used to lie through her teeth. (Following the accident, her behavior became far more violent as well.)For the nightmarish two-and-a-half years that she lived with us, my mother interfered with my life, my decisions, my child raising, my friends, and more. She always had to inject her advice and opinion, no matter if it was right or wrong. I cringed every time she had to put her two cents in. Although I did my best to cope with this very tough situation, I had no sense of belonging when my mother was there. I had no sense of freedom, no self-respect.

Soon after the birth of my first child, birth, I had a brainstorm. "Mom," I suggested gently. "Why don't you do yourself a favor? Why don't you go for a stay in Israel! You have amazing friends there. You can just go try it out for two or three months. If all goes well and you have a good time there, we'll rent an apartment for you. The baby and I will come visit you, of course, and then you'll come back with us to Miami if you'd like."

And that's the way it was. Mother left for Israel, and in no time I could see that she was doing great. Suddenly she was asking, "Do you mind if I have tea with my friends? Play cards?" I saw that she had her own life and friends. Perfect.

"Debbie, is it all right with you if I stay in Israel, or should I come back to Miami?" she asked me.

"Mom, of course I don't mind! Whatever is best for you! Why don't you keep the apartment in Israel for six months or a year? We can always extend it for another six months."

Amazingly enough, this arrangement turned out to be successful for us all. My mother lived happily in Israel, and we visited her there every so often. She would come back to visit us in Miami and stay with us for several months at a stretch. She came when my second daughter was born, and made frequent visits as the girls were growing up.

Recently I asked my oldest daughter what she remembers about growing up with "Nana." I'm still getting over one of the stories she told, which I had no inkling of until now.

"I was in around sixth grade or so when Grandma

would show up early at school to pull me and my sister out and get us ice cream," my daughter admitted. "After a while, I used to just go to the school office and call her to come get us!

"Nana was maybe fifty-nine or sixty at the time, but she looked older. She never came dressed, really, since she always wore a muumuu. The one I remember the most is a leopard muumuu that she'd wear, with her curly blond frizzy hair and her boobs hanging down. She'd show up in the brown Cadillac. She wasn't a very good driver (she was horrible), but we only lived two blocks away, so it wasn't so bad."

My daughters also have a vivid memory of my mom's cooking.

"I remember the Green Giant creamed spinach with mashed potatoes, the only food I'd agree to eat," my oldest daughter mused. "And I'll always remember the apple pie. But Grandma wouldn't give anybody the recipe. And she wouldn't allow any of us, including my mother, to be around her while she was making it. She actually kicked us out of the kitchen!"

Indeed, my mother's apple pie was the best I've ever had. Her secret ingredients came together to make a pie with a crust on the bottom filled with a layer of apricots, a layer of apples, and then sealed with dough on the top. She died with the recipe...

What I did not realize at the time was that my mother was becoming quite ill. I knew that her behavior was more nightmarish than ever, but I didn't put two and two together. All I could see was that whether she was with us in Miami or when I would come to visit her in

Israel with the kids, life was unbearable. She used to hit me repeatedly. Not physically, but verbally. I only hoped that the kids were too small to understand.

The blood clot in her brain was growing, and my mother's health seriously deteriorated. I began a grueling routine of leaving my husband and children to fly to Israel every six weeks or so to be with her.

At one point when my mother was hospitalized at the Hadassah Hospital in Jerusalem, something remarkable happened. I was at her bedside, and barely paid a glance to a woman in her thirties (like me) who was visiting the lady in the next bed. Fortunately, this visitor took a closer look at my mom and exclaimed, "Anita? Is that you?"

It was Ruthy Sherman, my best childhood friend and the one who had saved my life! Ruthy had remained in Colombia after I'd left for Miami, and we'd lost touch. She subsequently immigrated to Israel, and we found each other at long last right there in the hospital in Jerusalem.

As my mother's condition worsened, I put her in a nursing home in Israel and continued flying back and forth at short intervals. At the end of each visit when it was time for me to return home, Mother would say, "Why are you leaving now?" I'd tell her that I have small children. And she'd say, point blank, "But I'm more important than your children."

The guilt. She always tried to lay guilt on me. For my part, even after suffering a lifetime of her boldfaced cruelty, I still tried to find a way to make her love me.

My mother died on the day of my 39th birthday.

At the funeral and the shiva week of mourning, I never cried

We had just rented an apartment for the summer in Israel, and I remember that the balcony overlooked the cemetery in the mountains ahead. The whole summer I used to look directly towards her grave. I never shed even one tear.

My Dilemma

Bizarrely, my mother's death did not mark an end to her terrorizing my soul. She continued to torture me in my sleep and in my waking hours alike. The first time I went to a psychologist, he told me that I was the second-worst case he had ever seen, and that others like me would have long since committed suicide. He called me a survivor. But my dark secret is that the idea of suicide certainly crossed my mind. More than once.

The nightmares were relentless. Mother came to me again and again in my dreams, pinching me, hitting me, punching me and throwing me out of the house. I used to wake up in a cold sweat, but her spirit gave me no rest, hovering over me as a vast, poisonous cloud.

Like a woman possessed, I lit candles every night. I lit up lights and more lights to exorcise the demon. Early on, I went on a rampage seeking out things in my home which had belonged to my mother, just to get rid of them. All the antiques, very expensive items, all the dresses from every famous designer—Dior, Givenchy—I threw them all out. For the next decade, I don't know how I survived. I remained haunted by memories, lonely, depressed, and victimized. From the time I'd returned to Miami after my mother died, I couldn't be alone for a minute. Maybe my incessant need to be surrounded by people stemmed from her accusations that I was antisocial? I simply had to be with friends constantly, and I became very involved with my children.

I had to prove that I was the perfect person, when in essence I was the perfect actress. Over that decade, I delved into charity, which became a beacon of light for me in those dark days. I devoted my energy to helping WIZO, and soon became an inspiration for others, once I had something to live for outside myself. I was taking my first baby steps along the journey to discover the dark and light sides of my life. Yet, I ended up developing two personalities: by day, I could give and improve people's lives. By night, the demons engulfed me in terrifying, incessant nightmares. I asked a friend for help. I asked God for help.

Yet I found no peace, and I became more and more desperate. So desperate that my fiftieth birthday was nearly my last.

That birthday I just couldn't stop crying. Even the sheer beauty of a gorgeous sunny day atop Haifa's Mount Carmel could not soothe the pain of my broken heart. I'm fifty years old, and neither my husband nor my daughters had even thought to wish me well or send me a gift.

But who was I kidding? That wasn't what was really eating away at my soul. Ten years after my mother's death, I was still trapped into believing that I was inferior, unwanted, unloved. No matter how good my life really was, I could never enjoy its blessings without hearing my mother's angry voice putting me down, painfully hurting my "inner child" again and again.

My fiftieth birthday marked the crossroads. I peered down from the peak of Mount Carmel and knew precisely that there were only two paths open to me: to end my life by plunging here and now to the depths, or to soar all the way to the sky.

I took a long, hard look at the valley. Maybe it was the warm sunlight that helped me turn my gaze upward towards the heavens and say, "Dear God, is it time for me to end my suffering? Is there a reason for me to be here?"

Suddenly two white doves appeared before me from out of nowhere. A sign from God. It's time for you to soar. That was a moment of awakening and transformation on my spiritual journey. Not only suffering was a part of my being. I realized that I have a higher purpose in my life to fulfill. Only from the moment that I reached out for God's energy to be my guide, I was taught to believe in my higher self, connected with the Creator. I have a purpose in my life.

I haven't stopped flying since that day.

PART 3:
Easing the Journey
of Others

IX

Let Us Soar Together

By now, you've read my story, darkened by the profound pain and suffering I've described. Yet, as you will see, almost miraculously my life has been transformed to hold great peace, happiness and fulfillment. What follows is my gift to you: the key to finding the strength and inner peace that I have finally, gratefully achieved. The chapters that follow trace my experiences with the emotional and spiritual healing that have saved my life.

*A **spiritual encounter** changes a person's life, breathing new meaning, awareness and light that is virtually impossible to describe. I can't explain what precipitates the experience, or where its implications may reach. I can only tell you that these life-changing encounters, which transcend human understanding, have brought me the inner peace to rise above painful situations and to heal – and that you, too, can experience spiritual encounters that will light your way.*

These encounters go beyond human understanding. The more a person hurts, the more he or she searches for a higher purpose for the soul. When there is nothing left to lose, one can take the gamble. And choose to win. As in gambling, the willingness to enter into the unknown can be a frightening prospect. Yet I urge you to have no fear. A spiritual experience is a blessing that ultimately frees you to reach inner peace.

What I describe here are my own, very individual encounters. For you, my friends, I wish the freedom to

*embark on what is solely your own experience to reach a
higher plane and live life to the fullest.*

Gaining Strength

Soon after my spiritual encounter when the doves
appeared, I returned to Miami where I ran into a
friend who looked simply gorgeous. What was her
secret?

"I go to a great dietician named Andrea Larsen," she
told me. "I'll introduce you to her tomorrow because it's
my birthday. That will be my gift to you!"

Andrea is a skilled, expert nutritionist who taught
me how to eat healthy. I owe her a lot to this day. She
did an entire cleansing for me, a total body detox. All
the poison came out of my body.

I looked good, I felt good, but my soul still hurt.

"Andrea," I confided, "Do you know of a good psychologist who can guide and support me?"

"I have the best person in Miami!" she answered.
"Her name is Rosario Garrido, and she practices right
in my office complex."

The very next day I had the first appointment. I
walked in and said, "Hi, my name is Debbie Matzkin,
and this is me," as I recounted the brutal basics of my
life story.

Looking straight into my eyes, Dr. Garrido asked, "Do
you really want to heal yourself or are you just talking?"

"Absolutely yes," I blurted. "Believe me, I want to
heal myself and find out who and what I really am."

"OK," the doctor said slowly. "Now we are going to
start." And this was a turning point in my life.

"Sit back," Dr. Garrido ordered. "Close your eyes and imagine your favorite picture."

That was easy. My favorite picture has always sat right on my night table. It's a photo of me when I was one year old, holding onto the table in my grandparents' house. I'm tilting my face, and there's a tear falling from my eye.

"Do you see that little girl?" the doctor asked evenly. "Now you're going to talk to her. But first you're going to hug her. Make believe you're going to hug her."

At the very moment that I was about to hug this little girl, Dr. Garrido hurled a pillow at me, saying, "Grab the pillow, grab this little girl and tell her, 'Look how beautiful you are! Look what an amazing woman you are today! Look where you're going, look how a remarkable little girl flourished into the most beautiful woman!'"

At that point, I knew I was going to be okay. For a full year and a half, I didn't go anywhere. I stayed in Miami, and every Tuesday from 10:30-12:00 I would turn up promptly for my lifesaving sessions with Dr. Garrido. The time we spent together was always intense. Afterwards I'd be in and out, doing homework she gave me, discovering things, going places, finding myself. She helped me find who I was. And who I wasn't.

I could feel the confidence building up in my body at long last, giving me enough of a taste of strength to push me to seek even more.

That's when I knew it was time to solve the mystery of the two dreams that had consumed my consciousness and left mammoth questions gnawing away in my mind.

I was only four years old, but I can describe every vivid detail of my first dream as if I dreamt it last night. I'm in Egypt and I fall down through a hole into a huge, huge tunnel with white ceramic tiles, streaming with light. A river flowed there that teemed with water. I'm swimming through the tunnel and there's a crocodile behind me. I swim as fast as I can to escape him. At last, I crawl up through a hole and emerge in New York.

The second significant dream, which really changed my life, came when I was around eighteen years old: I'm in a dark, black space and out of the very, very black recesses a holy man emerges to walk towards me. He looks like the Biblical Moses, or perhaps a master. "Hold my hand," he tells me.

This Righteous Man then takes me to see how the universe was made. How the raindrops were formed, how the light was created, how a flower blossoms, how thunder clouds billow, how all components of the universe were made. And then he deposits me in a river of crystal-clear water with the most spectacularly beautiful, colorful fish. I feel nature, animals, flowers, life.

When I mentioned to a friend in Miami, Ora Bar, may her memory be blessed, how I often wonder about the meaning of my dreams, she invited me to join her at a lecture on the topic of analyzing dreams to be held at the "Kabbalah Center."

The lecturer, Eliyahu Yardeni, was phenomenal, opening my mind to a world of new discoveries and explanations of the meaning of dreams. But the most positive discovery of all was Eliyahu's wife, Yael Yardeni, one of the world's foremost authorities on charting astrological maps. I waited four months for an appointment with her. The awakening she gave me was beyond belief.

This famous astrologist bent steadfastly over each meticulously-charted segment of my personal map. As she slowly read its contents, she looked up at me and said carefully, "This is the fourth lifetime in which the souls of you and your mother have connected in destructive human encounters. To end this cycle, you must now go all the way back to the time that your mother appeared in your first lifetime. You must now release her towards the light. Otherwise, every time she comes to you, she will be worse and worse. Let her go."

On Yael's recommendation, I arranged an appointment with a Fort Lauderdale-based psychologist/kabbalist affiliated with the Kabbalah Center who specializes in Past Life Regression, which I'll soon explain in detail.

I could hardly concentrate on the cars passing me on either side as I made the one-hour trip from Miami to Fort Lauderdale. Briefed by Yael, the psychologist ushered me into her office.

Once again, I was asked the fundamental question: "Do you want to be healed?"

Yes, yes, yes. Every part of my being longed to be healed!

Then gradually my mind and my body surrendered to the peace and quiet surrounding me in that room. As the doctor brought my body to the point of total relaxation, I fell into a hypnotic trance, letting my subconscious take the reins, as the doctor began taking me back in time, further and further. When I reached 5,000 years ago in ancient Egypt (the scene of my first dream, and now my true awakening!), I saw who my mother was: a majestic queen. And she was already cruel to me, her child. The meaning of my first dream now became crystal clear to me.

"Cut the cord," the doctor told me. "The umbilical cord that attaches the two of you. Cut the cord! Then help her go up to the light."

As I severed the cord, a sharp pain actually crossed my belly, a crazy pain like a release. And then, through my imagination, I saw my mother's soul floating towards the light, smiling towards me and saying, "Thank you. And please forgive me."

When I opened my eyes at the end of this session, I broke into tears. The unbearable weight I'd carried for so long on my shoulders had entirely lifted! I looked out towards the sky and said, "Dear Lord, I am free! Thank you!" And I cried from sheer happiness. I don't remember if it was cloudy or sunny, but this was definitely one of the most beautiful days I'd experienced in my lifetime.

The first thing I did was to call my husband, who was in Israel at the time, to tell him, "I'm free!" And my life changed completely. Because at that moment I saw who I was. Who my soul is. Who I am in this world. Not my mother's child. I am not my thoughts. I am not my emotions. I am not my body. I am finally a free soul. This was the first awakening of my soul.

My real love of life came at that moment. I'd reached

true freedom. But if this really freedom, I asked myself, I wonder what will come next.

Looking To My Subconscious

In time, I delved further into that dynamic means to unlock an awareness of the power that lies within my soul: Past Life Regression Therapy, championed by Dr. Brian Weiss. As he wrote, "It is exhilarating when you realize how much greater you are than your current, confined ego or personality. The real you, the immortal you, is the you that is present from body to body, from life to life."

Several years back, I attended an Omega Institute Conference in Florida where Dr. Brian Weiss was the keynote speaker. In one of his exercises, I lay flat on the floor and began my hypnotic trance. First, I regressed to my mother's womb, and then I felt myself being whisked out of the auditorium by beings from a different world. Ultimately, they deposited me in a circular room where three pharaoh-like beings, the "Gods of Creation" were seated, correlating to my second dream. They communicated with me telepathically, telling me that my worries were over and that they would be guiding me on a spiritual level from that day forward.

"You are our key to making the universe a better place," they declared. "You are one of the oldest souls in this world. Through light, words of love and words of encouragement, you can bring a glimmer of hope to others."

I could hardly breathe for several days after this encounter. They had explained to me the power of life.

What's more, they made it clear that life did not start in this planet. There are many others in the universe....

This experience propelled me on a search for what we cannot see, what lies in the beyond. I needed to be aware of this, to pursue my soul's journey to discover the unknown. This marked my first initiation in understanding my path to enlightenment. I know myself. I found peace by knowing that all my pain was physical and emotional, but my soul was unscathed. Enduring the emotional pain was a vital lesson I needed in order to love myself as a human being.

Several years later, I visited the Yad Vashem Holocaust Museum in Jerusalem. As I reached the Auschwitz section, I was suddenly transported back in time. I found myself in the midst of the hell that was Auschwitz, where I could vividly smell the gas and sense the utter despair. I heard the piercing screams and felt the presence of six million souls. The experience was so overwhelming for my human conscious body that I fainted. I had to be carried out of Yad Vashem.

Soon afterwards, upon my return home to Miami late at night, there was a full moon in the sky, yet the room before me suddenly turned pitch black and freezing cold. Alone in the house, fully aware of the presence of something I couldn't see, I covered my eyes, covered myself, and fell into a troubled sleep.

The next day at the same time, the same drama reoccurred. I wasted no time in going to consult with a rabbi, who told me, "Thousands of souls of those murdered in the Holocaust have entered your house.

Please, you are the one they have been waiting for to help them see and reach the light."

I raced home that evening, filled a crystal glass with water and lit a candle, all the while reciting "Shma Yisrael, Hear, oh Israel, the Lord is One," and the powerful prayer Ana B'koach. I beseeched the souls around me, saying, "Your pain in this world is over. Go now to the Light. At last, you can rest."

Gradually I felt the light of love, the light of thanks and peace that poured steadily into my house.

I felt privileged and honored to be the one able to transfer these lost souls to their peaceful rest.

***

A Word from the Therapist:

According to metaphysical laws, there are different dimensions in a soul's journey to reach the Light. When a human encounters death, the soul does not die. It must traverse various levels of parallel dimensions to reach the final destination, the Creator.

If or when death was a traumatic event for the soul and the human consciousness, pieces of the soul may be so scattered that they cannot elevate the soul's transcendence to the light, and become trapped between dimensions.

When the soul meets an enlightened human being with a connection to his own soul, this person can become a portal to transfer the lost soul into the light.

***

I urge you to explore the metaphysical realm and discover how you are a part of this universe and other dimensions.

Every living soul has a sixth sense. Whether you want to use it or not depends on you.

It is easy to be skeptical and not to believe things you cannot see or understand. **But if you are willing to take a risk, to become aware of who you truly are – even if you must relive the traumas – you can understand your past and understand those who have wronged you. You can attain indescribable freedom.**

And what if your own past life regression brings you back to a life that is disappointing or even appalling? **Remember, you relive your past to better your future.** Regardless of where the regression takes you, there is always an opportunity for a better you in the future.

Who Made Me the Woman I Am Today?

Each child has one memory of who made him what he is today. In my case, the person who made me the very strong woman that I now am is none other than my mother.

Only after I learned to fully forgive her from the depths of my soul was I able to see how much I admired her.

Today I can say that in her own way, my mother was a remarkable woman with a multitude of talents, a high level of education, and a good number of lofty goals in her life. She was a pillar of society, the indefatigable head of the Bogota Garden Club and the city's International

Women's Club. She longed to reach a goal of meeting people worldwide, and be an amazing woman who made a difference.

My mother gave me a love for food, a love for people, a love for travel, and a love for culture. And for that I will always be grateful. Yes, yes, I saw the bad side she turned towards me, but also the greatness she showed towards the outside world. As for all the beatings and all the lying, ultimately I learned how to put them to the side and still grow from what I was learning from my mother.

I now know that you must separate the pain from the good. If you want to live a full life, you must learn to forgive, learn how to understand, and most important, learn to avoid judging others. **Therein lies the key: the moment you stop judging people and blaming others, you can take control of your own life.** That's the very point where you'll succeed in gaining respect for yourself, and others will respect you. You can now look forward to living your life to the fullest.

Which brings me to the crux of it all: my perception of love as being the essence of compassion and respect. Because without respect and compassion for a human being, there is no love. **Above all else in life, you must learn how to love and respect yourself.** To learn your own needs and fulfill them, and to set the proper borders.

Quite simply, if you don't fully love yourself, there is no place in your heart or soul to love anybody else.

I don't think my mother knew how to love herself. Most likely, this was a consequence of her upbringing.

I'm convinced that she pitied herself in many ways. She certainly never wanted to become a mother. She never wanted to remarry after becoming widowed at the age of thirty-seven. As I've shared, I suspect that she suffered emotional and perhaps physical abuse as a child. The mid-1900s in South America was an era marked by a multitude of taboos, where you could never talk or say anything about your past. You couldn't talk at all.

From the day I was born until the day she died, I never heard my mother utter the words, "I'm sorry." There was never a time that she could say, "I love you." So, unless you love yourself, perhaps there is no place within you to love anybody else. Even your one and only child. But when you do learn to love yourself, you understand the magnificent beauty that God gave you in this life and on this planet.

It's possible that my mother loved me in her way. My father loved me. But somehow, they didn't know how to show it. Neither kissed me. Yet, the scars are no longer there. That's my freedom. There are no scars. Instead, there are lessons to be learned.

I am very proud of who I am. And I am very proud of who I was. If I suffered, I don't ask why. I say thank you. Because the suffering is what made me the woman that I now am. My triumph is that I raised children who didn't need that suffering to become the wonderful, giving and loving people that they truly are.

For someone like me who was so profoundly abused, the notion of parenthood posed fearful threats. Would I automatically turn into my mother? Would the terrible cycle of abuse perpetuate itself? I remember making such a conscious effort to avert that scenario that at some point my daughters begged me, "Mom, don't kiss us and hug us so much. Please!"

I guess that in my children, I found the love I lacked from my own mother. Somebody once told me a wise sentence, "Once you heal yourself, you heal your children." Which is very true. Once I changed, I saw the difference in my children. And it's big time. When you respect yourself, then they respect themselves, and they respect each other all the more. When you admire yourself and become a better human being, they follow suit. Through my journey, I have been blessed to watch my children become so much stronger as we stride together, side by side. My greatest achievement is to have given them wings so they can fly.

My daughters were in their twenties when I healed myself. Better late than never! Through this book, I want them to feel proud of the legacy that I, their mother will leave behind. For them and their children, and their children's children, and all the children in the world, my message is simple and fervent: love yourselves, and love others. **Cherish life by treating each person in your world with respect and compassion.** This is the cycle you can and must perpetuate for generations to come.

The How-To's for Gaining Your Life Back
Looking at the tools I was given to regain my life, Dr. Rosario Garrido gave me one of the first and most effective ones: write four letters to myself at prescribed times. You can do this, too. **Write four letters to yourself. One is**

meant to be opened one year from now; the second letter to be opened in two years' time; the third in five years' time, and fourth in ten years' time. In each letter, you must describe the goals you've set for yourself and how you want to see yourself at that particular point in the future. Now keep these letters in a safe place, to be opened on the appointed dates.

There's no way to sneak a peek into the future, but once you've set viable goals and put them into writing, chances are that you'll actually give yourself a jump-start to reach those targets in good time.

After I wrote those letters, I can't tell you how thrilled I was to find myself reaching my five-year goal in only two years. That particular goal combined my passions: to appear on TV (and bring happiness to my viewers) and to take firm steps to bring peace to the world through love and food.

Food, after all, is the one entity that unites human-kind throughout the universe, and is the ideal medium to bring us closer to achieving universal peace. I'm convinced that both chefs and diners hold the key to advancing world peace, starting with sharing and exploring what they can teach one another from their own passions for food. Towards that aim, I work tirelessly to create international "food for peace" projects that promote these efforts to forge bonds on a worldwide scale.

As for the ideal backdrop to stage my entry into the world of television, I had no doubt that this show about glorious food and the people who create it would be "on location" in Israel, where we now live and work for several months of the year. I couldn't wait to show the world the wonders of Israel through a culinary journey. After all, Israel is the biggest and most pulsating melting pot in the world, the cradle of civilization and the world's three great religions. The perfect setting for a show, with so many different worlds all combined in the same country. Full of life! And love! And food!

Ever since I was a little girl, I've dreamed of being on TV. When I premiered my show, this was one unmistakably delightful proof that dreams can come true in a big way. The moment I saw myself on the screen, I whooped, "I did it! My way!" With no help from anybody, and despite my mother's biting criticism that met every initiative that I took, every step of the way in my formative years. **This has made me very happy and proud, and gives me the assurance to say that you, too, can definitely reach your goals. Even sooner than you think!**

But I must admit that a major element of my success was born of pure self-anger. One of my shortcomings that annoyed me most was my tendency to start something but never follow it through. The healing process opened the way for me to decide that come hell or high water, I would finish whatever I set out to accomplish. Today my philosophy is not to postpone a thing, to take risks in any endeavor, and to be extremely organized. Armed with those components, I dreamed up the idea to use the medium of a television series in order to best "merchandize" uniting the world through food.

My advice to you: lay a firm basis to launch the enterprise that defines your life's purpose. Then go for it!

Overcoming the Tragedies

Looking at my life, some people would say that I should have hated to get close to people. Because the more I loved, the more I lost and hurt. My beloved father, grandfather, great-uncle and aunt were snatched from my life when I was just a child (and needed them most).

Yet my own turning point came when I was around eighteen while attending university in Bogota. For one of my courses, I was assigned to report to a children's hospital and observe the clinical psychologist's work. I was in complete shock: for the first time in my sheltered life, I saw children who had been abandoned, and children who were physically handicapped. There was one little boy and a little girl who truly stole my heart. The boy was completely deformed. The girl was such a beautiful child. Her name was Angelica – my little angel. She had been abandoned, and I fell in love with her. To the point where I even asked my mother to adopt her. Of course, my mother said no. The next time I came to the hospital, they told me that this little angel had died. I was shocked and nearly inconsolable.

Somehow that tragic look at suffering and death triggered an understanding that straddled over into the larger events of my life. What is life, really? I don't know if that child had any love. Maybe the nurses loved her. I remember hugging her. I remember her smile. But I cried a lot when she died. And I said to myself, every single day I must thank God for what I have. I was devastated when my father, grandfather, great-uncle and aunt died, of course. But I thank God each day for every minute that I had with them. **Today I've learned**

to celebrate their lives. And to understand that each person represents a world within us. A world possibly unborn until this person arrives, and it's only through this meeting that a new world is born.

Just two weeks after the beautiful little girl's death, I was spirited out of Colombia to Miami's shores. One way or another, the total series of events caused a trauma that prevented me from being able to go back into a hospital to volunteer. Interestingly, many years later when I had my astrological map charted, the astrologist told me that now I needed to be part of a children's charity! As I mentioned, I was one of the founders of WIZO-USA, and today I'm active in Beit Ruth, an Israeli shelter for children-at-risk, not only for teenagers but for girls who have been abandoned and face heartbreaking challenges in their young lives. I understand them so well, and I'm grateful for the lessons that I can teach them.

True Happiness? It's Not What You Might Think

When I was young, my mother always told me that happiness is the key to life. When I went to school, they asked me what I wanted to be when I grew up. I answered, "Happy." They told me I did not understand the assignment. I told them they did not understand life.

More than other kids, perhaps, I cherished the happy moments that I had in my childhood, and certainly never took them for granted. But as I grew older, I sought new directions for attaining happiness. Like so many others, I was convinced that I needed many people in my life, but what I didn't realize was that I really needed quality, not quantity, in those who surround me. I felt that I needed to be accepted by everyone, instead of by the ones that matter.

Fortunately, a woman named Tania Busquela gave me a sentence to live by that changed my life. **"As long as you seek their approval, you will always be their prisoner,"** Tania warned me.

She was so right! Today I've reached the point that I really only need God's approval and my own approval to have a full life. Whoever does me wrong, their actions reflect on themselves, not on me. I only need my own approval to respect myself and to love myself, and to be loved and respected by others. My conscience is clear. I am happy. If you are miserable and you hate yourself, it shows on you more clearly than you can imagine. I now say to those who wrong me, "May God bless you and keep you far away from me." Never curse a person, only bless them.

And so, my heartfelt message to those of you who have suffered abuse and are trying to overcome the hurt, the shame, and the trauma is quite simple:

Don't judge. Learn to forgive. You may not know the full background of the one who is terrorizing you. Maybe that person was abused, or traumatized as a child, or a victim of war or strife. But once you learn to understand your tormentors as well as to understand their pain, then you learn how to forgive. And learn how to love.

Forgiving your abusive parent is such an extraordinarily complex and difficult assignment that it's hard to clearly see how to get there. I have a very close friend who frankly and sincerely declared to me that she had forgiven her mother. But I told her that she absolutely had not. Because from what she described and the way she talked, her mother is still very divisive and still manipulative. My friend would find no freedom until she could probe deep within herself to find the seed causing the dissention. And then remove it. You must learn how to do this, and here, from my own experience I urge you to seek the help of a therapist or counselor.

Another friend poured out her soul to me as we spoke for hours. She cried so bitterly and asked, "Was it my fault that my father and grandfather abused and raped me? Was it my fault?" she kept asking. But gradually she realized that the healing must begin somewhere. Within herself.

"No, no," she told me at last. "It really was not my fault!" And indeed, this opened the door to her healing. Once you understand the reason, your own blame disappears. The second you realize that you are not at fault, you are free. I can attest to this fact every waking (and sleeping) moment.

When Others Try to Hurt You

Like most everyone, I've sometimes been deceived by people I blindly trusted. Just recently, a "friend" caused so much anguish that I suffered physical pain. When a horrible rash developed on my face that would not heal, the last place I thought to search for a cure was — once again — a place deep inside me, buried by a toxic connection to my mother.

A string of coincidences (or not) led me to discover a phenomenal therapist, Arian Lev, whose wise observations I shared with you at the start of this book. Arian excels in healing the subconscious scars that plunge us into destructive relationships. In her research, she has discovered that the subconscious mind and the human brain are connected by an intricate network of codes, based on memories etched into our subconscious from utero through our first ten years.

Arian's analysis of these codes shows that the majority are positive in directing the brain to promote growth and development. But, 29 "blocking codes" prevent our inner strength from achieving positive goals, leading instead to frustration, pessimism and pain. When Arian carefully pinpointed those blocking codes that obstructed my subconscious, the trail led, naturally, to my mother's cold, crippling manipulations. Brilliantly, Arian led me to reprogram these codes — my emotional DNA — to empower me to move forward.

Indeed, I now realize that my so-called friend subconsciously reminded me of my mother, provoking the long-imbedded reaction that I "need to suffer." Not surprisingly, once I reached peace with myself and erased the lethal blocking code, the sores on my face healed without a scar.

At last, I understand that while in the past I may have released my mother, I didn't find myself. Until now.

You, too, must rid yourself of toxic relationships which ultimately poison your soul.

I urge you to seek treatment to enable you to discover and communicate with your inner self. Once again, if you cannot afford a professional, find a friend who will listen. That's the first crucial step.

No one has the right to humiliate you. No colleague, friend or partner has the right to hurt you.

Most, most important is that everyone can gain this freedom if they really want to. Go to a psychologist. Or go to a Karma therapist who does past-life regression. If you cannot afford professional care, I hope that you have a good friend who can listen to you. Open up! Don't be shy. **When you can begin to talk about the horrible secrets that you've suppressed, you're already opening up your inner being, peeling off the layers that are only strangling you.**

I promise that the moment you begin letting go of the terrible burden you bear, you will gain a measure of pride in yourself that is priceless. And I repeat, the moment that you love yourself, everything else will come.

I'm not sure I could love myself before I released my mother. I had to be ready to do it. It's just sad that I didn't have the backbone to confront my mother in her lifetime. Maybe I was living a lie? Or perhaps it's more about being scared, scared of confronting who you really are, scared of confronting life. Of saying to yourself that it's not your fault. Of being afraid to admit to yourself that you're an amazing person. It's a paradox of life that you don't know which way to take. You can continue being the victim, or you can let go and get your life back.

I remember closing my mother's eyes at her death. I whispered to her, "Now you can go in peace. I love you and I forgive you. And please forgive me for whatever I did." Once I forgave and asked for forgiveness, I began to gain the strength to be the strong woman that I am today.

Perhaps the one major regret that I have in life is not having forgiven my mother long before. I should have taken responsibility and sought out the proper help many years before I actually did. On the other hand, perhaps I was not ready and the time wasn't right. But whatever regrets I may have, they certainly contributed to my drive to get where I am today.

I protected myself all those years. To this day, my friends don't know the hell that I went through. But I know that my mother was not at peace, whether because she herself was an abused child or for some other reason that I will never discover.

Today I pray to God that wherever she is, my mother has found the peace that she so deserved. In a leopard-colored muumuu, and free as the wind.

Acknowledgement

Thank you to the therapists who led and taught me:
Dr. Brian Weiss, for making me aware that there are other paths to take to heal my soul;
Andrea Larsen, for making my body as my temple;
Dr. Rosario Garrido, for starting my soul's journey to recovery
Arian Lev, for helping me reconnect to my soul

I thank **Valda Tair Ozeri**, my spiritual counselor, for showing me how to stay on my path;
My editor **Melanie Rosenberg**'s words touched my soul. Thank you for helping me express them.

To God Almighty my Creator, I am grateful for the courage and strength You have given me to embark on my journey through life.

Above all, I thank my family for the support and love I needed to reach my destination.

About the Author

Globally-noted businesswoman, culinary expert and humanitarian **Debbie Matzkin** began her life's journey in Bogota, Colombia, and now resides in Tel Aviv and Miami. In *Surviving My Mother,* she shares her intriguing life adventures while disclosing the long-hidden sexual abuse that began in childhood.

Debbie Matzkin's revelations and careful guidance are vital for all who strive to live life to the fullest.

Tribute:

"Debbie Matzkin is not only a culinary genius, but also a woman with a giant heart and beautiful soul. Her insights on life can be invaluable to her readers."

Dudu Fisher,
world-renowned singer
and Broadway performer

My Dynasty

My great great grandmother, 1879

My great grandmother
as a baby

My great grandparent's wedding,1894

My Dynasty

Some of my grandmother's
best friends in Austria

My grandfather in the Austrian army 1916

My Grandmother

My grandmother Hedwig (Hedwly) Wexcler

My grandparents house, Bogota Colombia,1950

My Grandfather

My grandfather Herman (Von Reich) Finkelman

My grandfather in the Austrian army

My Parents

My father and his parents in Karlovi Vari

My father in school Viena, 1927

My father and his mother

My Parents

My father and my grandparents with Charles 1st Emperor of Austria
and Otto Von Hapsburg

My grandmother
Golda Finkelman & my mother

My grandmother
Golda Finkelman & my mother

My Parents and Me

My Perent's Wedding 1947

My parents going out for dinner

My parents and me

Sad Baby Girl

Me at my first birthday

My mother and me on my
second birthday

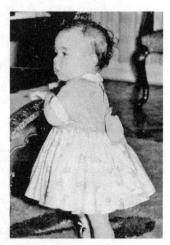

The pictures of me hanging
onto the table and crying

My Father and Me

My father and me in Salzburg

My father and me

The day I was taken to boarding school in Switzerland

The day my mother told me "I wish, you were never born"

My best friend Debby May

My Aunt Ruthy

My mother's sister Ruthy,
she saved my life

My aunt Ruthy,
my mother's sister

My class picture, together with my friends:
Chachi Stern, Jaime Demner, and Ruthy Sherman

Marriage

Giora and me on Our wedding day 9.7.1978

On the seashore in Miami

My Life in Miami

In one of the many charity
events we attended

One of the many Charity balls,
Miami

Miss Universe Gala ceremony

My initiation to the international woman club

Visiting the USA Army & Navy in Japan

Under Mt. Fuji, Japan

Trophies and Friends

Receiving the woman of the year award from City
of Hope with President Rhoda Ehrlich

Winning the bake off in the USA

Rivka Eliani and Dina Gershoni, my friends who introduced
me to Marrocan food and made me love it

Around the World

In front of Tut Ankh Amon tumb

Geisha house Kyoto

My love and passion
for Egept tour

Made in United States
North Haven, CT
26 August 2023

40781240R00088